Everyday Nature Secrets

DISCOVER THE HIDDEN WORLD IN YOUR BACKYARD

CONTENTS

A Birds & Blooms Book

1610 N. 2nd St.,
Suite 102,
Milwaukee, WI
53212-3906

Illustrations throughout
Katy Dockrill (drawings); Getty Images: Angelina Bambina; marabird; MaryliaDesign; Taisiia Iaremchuk (accent shapes)

Front cover photo credits
Getty Images: César Martínez Amor (squirrel); John A. Anderson (butterfly); Larry Keller, Lititz Pa. (bird); OlgaMiltsova (flowerpot)

Back cover photo credits
Martin Poole/Getty Images (produce); mirceax/istock (bird); Design Pics Inc/Alamy Stock Photo (butterfly)

ISBNs
978-1-62145-820-3 (dated)
978-1-62145-857-9 (undated)
978-1-62145-821-0 (retail)
978-1-62145-854-8 (e-pub)

Component Numbers
119500100S (dated)
119500102S (undated)

We are committed to both the quality of our products and the service we provide to our customers. We value your comments, so please feel free to contact us at TMBBookTeam@TrustedMediaBrands.com.

For more Birds & Blooms products and information, visit our website:

www.birdsandblooms.com

Text, photography and illustrations for *Everyday Nature Secrets* are based on articles previously published in *Birds & Blooms* magazine.

Printed in China
10 9 8 7 6 5 4 3 2 1

AMY BOSSE

Your Journey Starts Here

You've always lived in the company of nature. But have you lived in true companionship with it?

As you page through this book (best enjoyed while sitting outside on your favorite chair), you'll start to do exactly that. We've designed it as a resource, packed with information on what makes nature and its creatures so incredible. But, above all, we've created it so you feel a deeper connection with all the blooming, buzzing, fluttering and flying happening around you.

Feel free to jump in anywhere. Read a little section or two, get inspired and maybe even grab your binoculars. Then do it again the next day. This is your journey. We hope it's a colorful one.

—*The editors of* Birds & Blooms *magazine*

CHAPTER 1

Your Backyard as Nature's Home

LOOK OUTSIDE. IT'S AMAZING WHAT BIRDS AND BUTTERFLIES ARE UP TO—AND WHAT YOU CAN DO AS THEIR HOST.

For nature's creatures, the outside world is home sweet home. And your backyard is one big living room. It's time to explore how birds and wildlife use their green, leafy spaces. We'll reveal how you can be a good neighbor to them. You'll even learn how to spot different types of nests and get tips on how to draw your favorite fliers closer than ever before.

Great spangled fritillary on purple coneflower

10 WAYS TO BUILD AN ABODE FOR BUTTERFLIES

It's easier than you think to bring these vibrant, fluttery fliers to your yard.

1 Don't get too hung up on the size of your garden or how fancy it looks. Butterfly gardening can be as small as a few pots on your back porch. Remember that the best butterfly gardens can look a little overgrown or ragged—that's enticing to the butterflies.

2 ◀ PROVIDE GOOD FOOD SOURCES. Most butterflies get the majority of their diet from nectar-producing plants, so these should make up the largest part of your garden. Good bets for almost anyone include salvia, lantana, pentas, aster, marigold, zinnia and coneflower.

3 Let go of chemicals. Gardeners should avoid using pesticides, herbicides and fertilizers that have harmful effects. Prep your butterfly garden's soil with plenty of compost so your plants will thrive without much additional fertilization. If you need to kill off grass in the area, cover it with a layer of newspaper, cardboard or weed cloth and add about 4 inches of mulch on top.

CAROL L. EDWARDS

4 Put non-plant options on the menu. Some butterflies, like mourning cloaks and red-spotted purples, prefer to feed on tree sap or rotting fruit. Offer fruit like bananas, strawberries and oranges for these butterflies. Keep ants away by filling a shallow dish with water and setting the fruit in the middle.

5 Include host plants. Butterflies need places to deposit their eggs, and each species has a plant or group of plants that their caterpillars will eat, known as host plants. The best way to attract a wider variety of butterflies is to provide the host plants they need.

DAVE WELLING

Giant swallowtail on coneflower

6 Make room for milkweed. Host plants vary by area, but just about anyone can plant milkweed for monarchs, hollyhocks for painted ladies and violets for great spangled fritillaries.

7 Create your own "puddles." Butterflies use their delicate proboscises to sip water from dewdrops and puddles. Some are especially likely to gather in large numbers around muddy areas. Go ahead and try to mimic these natural water areas with a shallow dish of wet sand or mud.

Black swallowtails on lantana

Monarchs on garden phlox

8 **Do a little research.** To determine the best host plants for your garden, start by finding out which butterflies are regular visitors to your area. Then start seeking out the host plants these butterflies need.

9 **Offer natural "butterfly houses."** Raindrops can seem like bowling balls to butterflies, so when bad weather threatens, they seek shelter. Though you can buy ready-made butterfly houses, you'll find butterflies are likely to use natural areas such as tall grasses and thick shrubs.

10 **Let fall leaves lie.** Some butterflies overwinter in crevices in tree bark and rocks, while others spend the winter as caterpillars or chrysalides buried deep in the leaf litter beneath trees. Don't be too quick to remove all that fallen foliage each autumn.

LEFT: RICHARD DAY/DAYBREAK IMAGERY; RIGHT: KITCHIN AND HURST/GETTY IMAGES

Northern cardinal

BRING IN THE CARDINALS

Follow these quick tips and you'll have a backyard full of scarlet fliers.

Grab some cover. A yard with plenty of cover is likely to host many cardinals (especially in winter, when these birds travel in flocks); try planting arborvitae, juniper and spruce.

Stock the pantry for new cardinal families. It's easy: Plant caterpillar host plants like dill, fennel, hollyhock, mustard greens and snapdragon. Parent cardinals feed their young almost exclusively with insects; when very young, babies eat soft-bodied insects such as caterpillars.

Plant raspberry, hawthorn, sumac and winterberry. They help males shine bright red. For a male, the more vibrant his red, the likelier he is to find a mate. Males must eat a variety of bright red foods to keep their coats glowing.

Grow medium-sized seeds. Aside from filling your feeders with black oil sunflower seed, try planting corn, Purple Majesty millet, nasturtium, purple coneflower, safflower, sunflower and sweet pea.

▼ CONSIDER NESTING HABITS

Help cardinals raise their brood in peace. You can do it by offering box elder, eastern red cedar, hawthorn, nannyberry, rose and wild grape. Cardinals build their nests only 4 to 8 feet off the ground, and they prefer the coverage of and protection of evergreens.

MICHAEL ABEL

Female cardinal

Red-headed woodpeckers

OPEN HOUSE

Knock, knock. It's time to take a peek inside four of the most common bird homes.

◀ NEST CAVITIES. Instead of creating a traditional nest, woodpecker species like downies and hairies carve out a nest cavity within a tree. Males and females take turns using their bills to dig and then line the bottom of the 6- to 15-inch-deep cavity with soft wood chips.

Cup-shaped nests. These are the most common types found in backyards. Birds like American robins and blue jays build their cup nests on branches or ledges with twigs, grasses and sometimes man-made materials such as string, cloth and paper.

JULI WELLS

Late Nesters

Watch for these birds nesting as late as August and September.

MOURNING DOVES
They'll raise as many as six broods in a season! They don't use traditional birdhouses, but they will nest in hanging baskets.

EASTERN BLUEBIRDS
They may have three or more broods in a season, so keep watching your nest boxes.

AMERICAN ROBINS
They can still be laying eggs in August. Put out a nesting platform instead of a birdhouse.

Huge flat nests. Several species construct large and somewhat flat nests on platforms and in trees. The birds interweave large sticks, moss and grass to create these nests. One pair of bald eagles will reuse the same nest, which can eventually weigh up to 2 tons, every year.

▶ GOURD-SHAPED POUCHES

Orioles like Bullock's, Baltimore and Altamira gather fibers, including twine and string, to create gourd-shaped pouches hanging from branches. The female oriole works on the nest from the inside and forms the bottom to the shape of her body.

Black-capped chickadee

NEST BOXES TO KNOW

Welcome more bird families to your backyard by offering cozy places to raise young.

◀ SONGBIRD HOUSE

Chickadees, titmice, bluebirds and wrens are the most common backyard cavity nesters. They take up residence in classic wood birdhouses, but they're very particular about the size of the entrance hole. So get precise: These songbirds are most likely to raise a family in a box if the hole is 1⅛ to 1½ inches in diameter.

Woodpecker house. Entice woodpeckers with boxes attached to tree trunks, anywhere from 8 to 12 feet high. Add 4 inches of wood shavings to the floor—woodpeckers use it as nesting material. The preferred entrance hole size varies by species. Downies like 1¼ inches; flickers favor 2½ inches.

▲ SCREECH-OWL HOUSE

Hang a house for screech-owls to nest in the summer and roost in winter. They will use a box with an elliptical entrance hole 4 inches wide by 3 inches high. Watch them peek their heads out around dusk. Bonus! Wood ducks are attracted to the same type of birdhouse.

Purple martin house. Purple martins nest in colonies, so to attract them, consider a six- to 12-cavity house. Being a martin landlord takes commitment. First set up the large multiunit house 12 to 18 feet above ground—and then keep the cavities clear of nonnative house sparrows.

Your Nesting Questions, Answered

Experts Kenn and Kimberly Kaufman explain how many eggs in your birdhouse is normal and how to keep wasps away.

Q Usually robin nests in my yard have three eggs, but last year I saw eight. Is that normal or are multiple robins using the same nest?

—Sommer Raines
Connersville, Indiana

KENN AND KIMBERLY: When robins find a good site for a nest, they sometimes come back and use it repeatedly, as you've seen. But they typically lay three or four eggs, seldom a clutch of five. When a nest holds six to eight robin eggs, two females probably are laying eggs in the nest—perhaps competing for the site until one gives up. So what you have found is truly unusual, and it's an example of the fascinating discoveries that come with careful observation.

Q How do I keep wasps out of my birdhouses so that the birds can actually use them?

—Marge Berger
Necedah, Wisconsin

KENN AND KIMBERLY: Wasps will certainly take advantage of the shelter nest boxes provide. If they do move in, remember that they are beneficial pollinators, and don't use pesticides on them. Fortunately, there's a simple way to prevent them from taking up residence in nest boxes in the first place. Rub the inner roof of the top of the box with bar soap to create a slippery surface. It won't harm the birds, but then the wasps can't attach and build their hanging nests there.

BIRDBATH BASICS

For a robust bird population, just add water. Lure more species to your backyard with these tips.

Your feathered friends won't mind if you recycle. Give a trash can lid, old pan or flowerpot tray new life as a quick and easy birdbath.

Clean and rinse your bath every couple of days and then add fresh water. Grab a wire brush for a deep clean if algae forms.

Nestle baths in a shady spot (to keep water fresh) that is near trees or shrubs, but not so near that predators can lurk in ambush. When a bird is taking a dip and a predator flies by, it needs a safe and somewhat hidden place.

Place rocks or stones in the middle of your bath for birds to perch and drink without getting their feet wet.

▼ MOTION

Add motion with a dripper, fountain or mister. The noise and movement catches a bird's attention better than standing water. Bonus! Hummingbirds love a light mist!

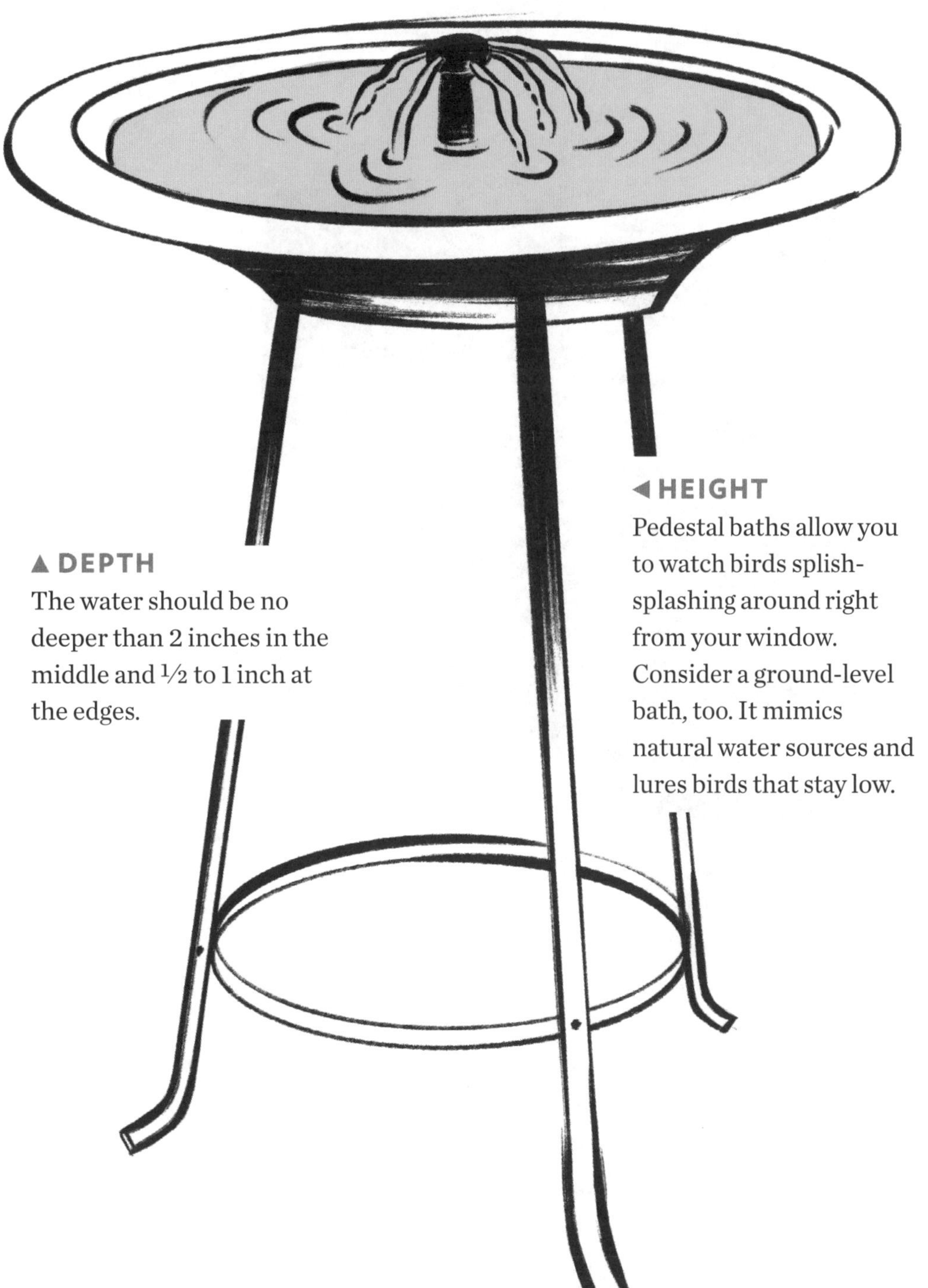

▲ DEPTH

The water should be no deeper than 2 inches in the middle and ½ to 1 inch at the edges.

◀ HEIGHT

Pedestal baths allow you to watch birds splish-splashing around right from your window. Consider a ground-level bath, too. It mimics natural water sources and lures birds that stay low.

American robin

Field Notes

Bath Time

An American robin came to play in the water of a small birdbath on my back deck. It dipped its head in the water and turned around and around. The bird had fun splashing and making water droplets fly. I snapped several photos, hoping to capture the water movement as well as the motion of its wings.

—Mary Jo Mantey
Port Austin, Michigan

Reader Secrets: Get a Cleaner Birdbath

Our community has a few tricks to keep your basins fresh and backyard birds healthy.

I have a designated toilet brush that I use with a spritz of diluted bleach cleaner. After scrubbing, I just rinse and refill. The brush is handy for getting into the small openings in the bath heater, too.

—Vanessa Lazar
Exeter, New Hampshire

Shake baking soda into the basin. It removes mold easily and is safe for birds.

—Stephen Holland
Sandown, New Hampshire

In the Florida heat, slime forms quickly. I avoid chemicals or soaps around the birds, so I hose my birdbath down with a power washer.

—Kathryn Rucci
Orlando, Florida

Good old dish soap and a scrubber gets the job done.

—Darcy Larum
Janesville, Wisconsin

Cleaning the birdbath isn't my favorite task, but it's more fun when you use baking soda and white vinegar. The foam reaction is neat to watch and makes cleaning easy.

—Sharon Erdt
Chester, Virginia

My pedestal is hollow, so I store a scrub brush on a wire below the birdbath. I dump out the water, scrub the bath, rinse and refill. Voila!

—Sheryl Smyth
Clinton, Tennessee

"I value my garden more for being full of blackbirds than of cherries, and very frankly give them their fruit for their songs."

—JOSEPH ADDISON

Bohemian waxwing munching on winterberry

Dahlia

PLANTING FOR POLLINATORS

Whether you love watching bees or run from them, a simple fact remains: They're important. Bees look for pollen and keep our ecosystem blooming. There are many pollinating plants that will entice bees to your garden. If you don't mind your yard abuzz, plant these all-star pollinators.

◀ **DAHLIA**

***Dahlia* spp., Zones 8 to 11.**

With a little extra work, dahlias thrive almost everywhere. Most cultivars do best with loads of sun and monthly low-nitrogen fertilizer treatments. In colder climates, dig up the tubers each fall and replant in early spring.

Lavender

***Lavandula* spp., Zones 5 to 10.**

Watch bees, painted ladies and hummingbirds frequent this fragrant plant from June to August. It grows best in gardens with loose, sandy soil, making it a perfect fit for most rock gardens. Harvest the stalks for an aromatic centerpiece or dry them for potpourris.

JAY GALVIN

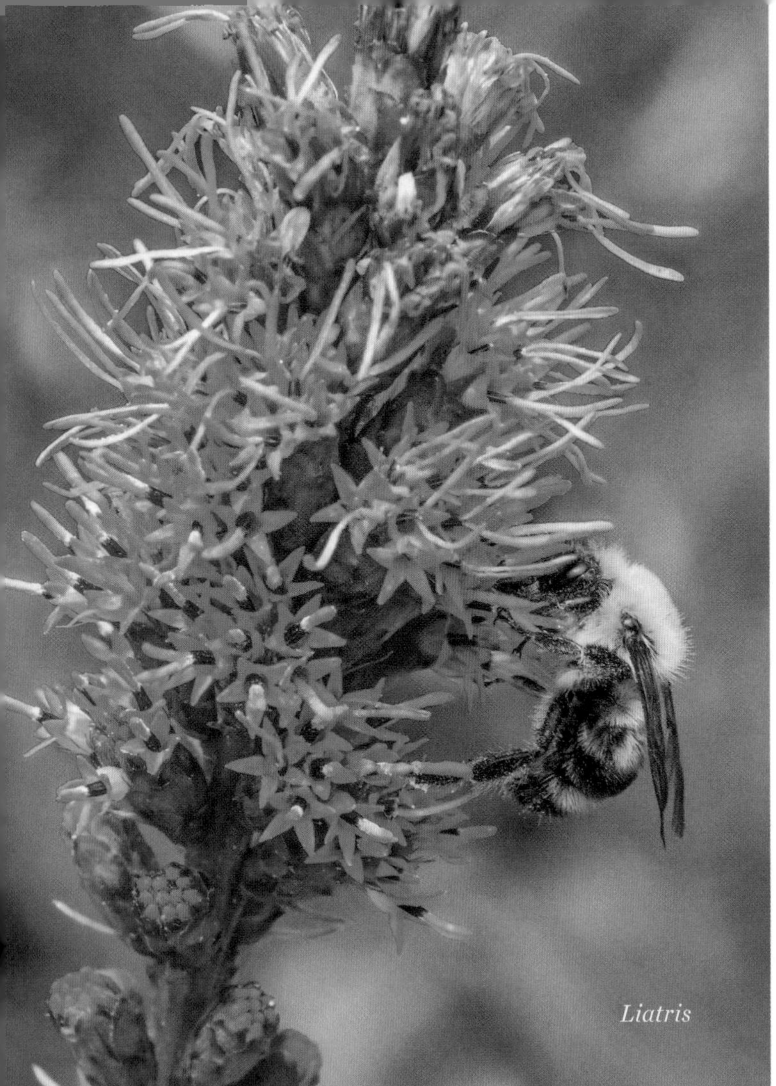
Liatris

◀ LIATRIS
Liatris spicata,
Zones 3 to 8.
Topping out at 4 feet tall, towering liatris offers a magnificent pollen buffet for butterflies and bees. Flower spikes range from purple to white and feature dozens of blooms.

Rose Of Sharon
Hibiscus syriacus,
Zones 5 to 9.
In the right conditions, this upright shrub reaches 12 feet tall, creating an excellent privacy screen or focal point. The large tropical-looking flowers add flair to yards from July to September.

Poppy
***Papaver rhoeas,* Annual.**
Sometimes known as corn or field poppy, this flower grows in many areas of the U.S., although its prolific self-seeding makes it invasive in some regions. The blooms thrive in well-draining soil.

Indian blanket

◀ INDIAN BLANKET
***Gaillardia pulchella*, Annual.**
These tough growers thrive virtually anywhere. Red, yellow or bicolor flowers burst to life in late spring and last until fall. Seeds may be difficult to find in garden centers but are available online.

Aster
***Aster* or *Symphyotrichum* spp., Zones 3 to 10.**
These garden all-stars begin blooming in late summer, providing lasting color through fall. No matter which hue you choose, bees and butterflies are sure to flock to their daisylike flowers.

Vitex

***Vitex negundo,* Zones 6 to 9.** Often called a chaste tree, this blooming shrub grows to more than 10 feet tall in warm winter climates and 3 to 5 feet tall in cooler regions. Its gray-green leaves complement small, fragrant flowers that pollinators love.

Salvia

***Salvia spp.,* Zones 3 to 11.** Gardeners can choose from a long list of salvia varieties—and the benefits that come with them. These purple, pink, red, white or yellow tube-shaped flowers are attractive to most hummingbirds and pollinators.

Bloodroot

***Sanguinaria canadensis,* Zones 3 to 8.** Bloodroot pops up in rich woods and along streams in early spring. Plant this flower to naturalize shaded wooded areas. The rootstock is poisonous, so be cautious growing it around children or pets.

▼ VERONICA

***Veronica spp.*, Zones 3 to 8.**

Also called speedwell, veronica bursts with blooms May through July. Their flower spikes grow about a foot tall in a range of colors and growth habits, and—with the proper trimming—may come back for a second bloom in late summer.

Veronica

STEFFANI PITZEN

Blue jay

DEBORAH MORRISON

Field Notes

Grabbing dinner

Taken in my yard over the summer with a Canon EOS 5D Mark III, this blue jay image stands out as one of my best. I was shooting birds in flight when this jay leaned forward. I was expecting it to take off, but it turned out that the jay was just waiting to have dinner delivered.

—Deborah Morrison, Bowerston, Ohio

13 WAYS TO BE A BIRD'S BEST FRIEND

You can be a BFF to birds—just ask an enthusiast. Here are tested and true backyard tips for buddying up to birds of all kinds.

1 **Water, food and shelter!** Any one of them is a solid start, but combine all three and more birds than ever will call your backyard home. Then, the next step is to vary your feeders by location, seed type and height.

—Kathy Eppers, Aledo, Texas

3 **If you're new** to watching birds, pick up an illustrated field guide and keep it near a window that looks out on your feeders. I keep my copy of *Birds of North America* from St. Martin's Press near my favorite window—it's always there when I need it.

—Sydra Krueger, Bay City, Michigan

2 ▶ **VARIETY ACT**

Different foods attract different birds, so make sure you're offering as wide a variety as possible. For example, right now, I am serving thistle for the goldfinches, sugar water for the hummingbirds, jelly for the orioles, and several types of high-fat suet blocks for the woodpeckers.

—Roberta Klein, Byron, New York

GAP PHOTOS

A yellow-breasted chat gets a calorie boost from a beautyberry shrub.

RICHARD BUQUOI

4 ◀HIDING OUT Tall shrubs (about 10 to 15 feet high) invite birds like robins and cardinals to build their nests in the safety of the dense foliage. Your new bird neighbors will be in a more secure space and farther away from predators.

—Sharon Blumberg, Munster, Indiana

5 Leave bushes bushy to provide shelter for birds. Consider putting up branches and perches near the feeders to act as "waiting rooms" for those times when all the feeder slots and perches are taken.

—Sue Cassidy, Hughesville, Maryland

Ruby-throated hummingbird

6 ▲ **SPRAY AND PLAY**
Birds love water. And it's a necessity, especially in winter. My neighborhood fliers are drawn in by the sound of splashing water from the waterfall in my backyard pond. I also have several heated birdbaths.

—Boni Trombetta, West Chester, Pennsylvania

7 **Protect the backyard** birds you've worked hard to attract by always keeping pet cats indoors. It's better for the overall health of your beloved cats, too!

—Judy Roberts, Graytown, Ohio

8 **In January, I** go to my local public works department, where people dispose of their Christmas trees. I find some really full ones and place them around my feeders for shelter during the rough winter months to come. (I check for any leftover and potentially harmful decorations or hooks first, though.)

—Patty Dorsey, North Huntingdon, Pennsylvania

LISA SWANSON

9 Provide lots of backyard shelter, including shrubs and trees, and feed black oil sunflower seeds or a black oil heavy mix. I feed the birds in both squirrel-proof and non-squirrel-proof feeders, so even those backyard critters get to eat.

—Grace Huffman, Oklahoma City, Oklahoma

10 Offer water year-round. For the sake of insect-eaters, such as grosbeaks, hummingbirds and bluebirds, skip the pesticides. Hungry birds help control insect populations, and many bird species switch almost exclusively to insects while feeding their nestlings because insects are a protein source. And leave up spiderwebs when you see them—hummingbirds use the webs to build nests.

—Jill Staake, Tampa, Florida

11 One simple way to help mother birds is to leave out eggshells, which give them a nice calcium boost. Every night I eat an egg for supper, I rinse out the shell to let it dry. I break it up and leave it outside my kitchen door for the birds to peck at in the morning. The blue jays especially seem to love it!

—Roger Emerick, South Glastonbury, Connecticut

JOHANN SCHUMACHER DESIGN

Eastern bluebird with juniper berries

12 Sugar-water feeders are especially tricky to clean. Recently, in a moment of inspiration, I grabbed my old electric toothbrush, put in some fresh batteries and had a blast getting all the gunk out from around all those itty-bitty holes in the feeder.

—*Liza Marie, Santa Rosa, California*

13 ◂ **SNACK BREAKS** Research native plants and trees. I grow a lot of native flowers, and after they finish blooming, their heads offer seeds that goldfinches and other seed-loving birds can't resist. The same idea applies with berry trees. Cardinals and cedar waxwings are sure to stop by for a sweet berry snack. If you're patient, attracting birds with your garden makes for many amazing photography opportunities.

—*Connie Etter, Martinsville, Indiana*

HOW TO KEEP HUMMINGBIRDS COMING BACK

There's nothing more magical than catching a glimpse of a tiny, jeweled flier. Why not entice them to make a pit stop at your house? Avid birders reveal how.

Keep your feeders at the ready to support early birds and late arrivals! I usually hang my feeders as early as St. Patrick's Day and take them inside on Halloween.

—Rochelle Backer,
Arlington, Tennessee

Make your own nectar. My birds seem to like the homemade stuff a lot more than mixes.

—Jackie Taylor,
Hubert, North Carolina

If your hummingbirds are aggressive, it's best to place several feeders around your yard, preferably in the corners so territorial birds won't be able to guard all the feeders at once.

—Toni Hall,
South Lake Tahoe, California

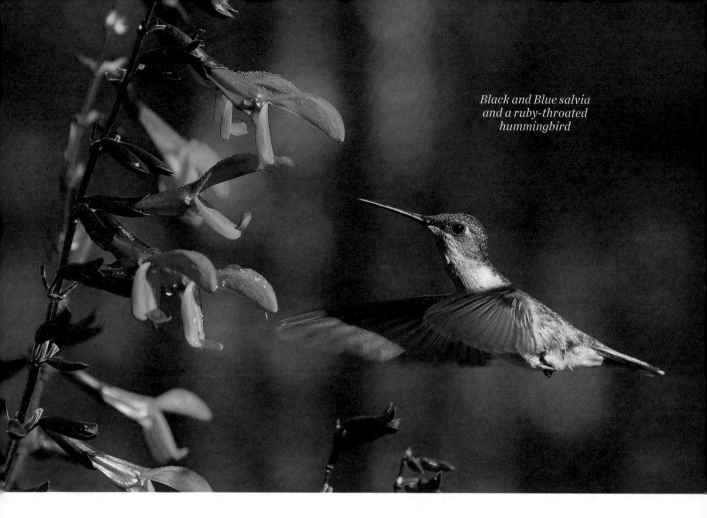

Black and Blue salvia and a ruby-throated hummingbird

I use saucer feeders because they're easy to clean and don't drip.

—Becky Sims, Montague, California

The best way to attract hummingbirds is to keep feeders clean. Use only boiled water and sugar, and hang feeders in shady areas so the nectar doesn't spoil.

—Barbara Wilkinson, Golden, Colorado

▲ BEST FLOWER

Plant sweet peas or Black and Blue salvia under a window for a natural food source. They love darting from flower to flower.

—Carolyn Lennart, Warrenville, Illinois

BACKYARD TALES

HOW A BIRDER MADE HUMMINGBIRDS FEEL AT HOME

A dream of finding an active nest came true for expert Kimberly Kaufman.

Ruby-throated hummingbird nest

KIMBERLY KAUFMAN

In the East, there's one breeding hummingbird species, but it's a good one! Ruby-throated hummingbirds are real charmers. These tiny birds have so much attitude and charisma that it definitely makes up for the lack of hummingbird diversity in our region.

When my husband, Kenn, and I got married and moved into our first home, it didn't seem likely that there would be many birds nesting in our yard, let alone a hummer. The house was in the country, but it was surrounded on all sides by the monoculture of farm fields: mostly corn, wheat and soybeans. Our landscape had a few mature trees, including maples and pines, but not much else to entice a discerning bird looking for a place to raise its young. But we hung our feeders and hoped.

Hummingbirds found our feeders, and we were thrilled. But to be honest, we never even thought of looking for a nest. Then one afternoon while we were in the backyard, a hummer buzzed by and flew into one of the pines. We

Ruby-throated hummingbirds

WILLIAM LEAMAN/ALAMY STOCK PHOTO

stood in utter astonishment as she began to work on what appeared to be the makings of a nest! Kenn dashed for the scope, and we spent the next four hours watching this industrious little fairy as she labored to create her haven.

What female hummingbirds lack in size they make up for in productivity. Males do not take part in nesting at all, so the females do all the work, building the nest, incubating the eggs and raising the young.

And speaking of the tiny nest, what an amazing example of miniature architecture! From the day we discovered "our" female beginning to build the nest, it took six days for her to finish the mini masterpiece. The list of building materials sounds more like a spell from a Harry Potter book than nest material. Spiderweb and plant down are covered with carefully selected lichens, stuck to the nest exterior to help camouflage both the structure and the young.

After watching for many hours, I finally surrendered to the call of duty and went inside to get some work done. Half an hour later, Kenn came rushing into the house with a dazed look on his face saying, "You've got to come out and see this."

Outside—in the front yard this time—was another nest! Less than 30 yards from the one she was constructing in the backyard, our little overachiever had herself another nest (yes, it was the same female), and this one was filled to capacity with two stubby-billed, adorable baby hummers.

I am not ashamed to admit that I cried. It was so spectacularly magical to have not one but two hummingbird nests in our small yard—and to discover them on the same day. The realization that this tiny bird would be actively building another nest while raising two demanding "kids" at the same time—all on her own—was such emotional overload for me.

It was the best day.

MONICA HALL

Ruby-throated hummingbird

A white-lined sphinx moth hovers near foxglove in Texas Hill Country.

"Study nature,
love nature, stay
close to nature.
It will never
fail you."

—FRANK LLOYD WRIGHT

ROLF NUSSBAUMER

CHAPTER 2

Why Do Birds Do That?

BIRD BEHAVIOR IS EVER FASCINATING. NOW, YOUR BIGGEST QUESTIONS ARE ABOUT TO BE ANSWERED.

How do such small creatures make such lengthy journeys? What traits do they want in mates? And why, oh why, do they break into song right at dawn? Find out, plus discover how to track migration patterns and get tips on feeding and keeping bird bullies at bay. It's all in the spirit of getting to know our feathered friends a bit better.

American robin

SINGING LOUD FOR ALL TO HEAR

Whether you can identify your avian pals by ear or you simply appreciate their cheery ditties, there's plenty to love—and learn—about bird songs and calls.

If you record a simple birdcall and slow it down, you will discover all kinds of details there that your ears didn't hear. Other birds probably can hear these extra sounds—otherwise, birds would have no reason to make them.

◂ ALWAYS LISTENING
In some species (including virtually all flycatchers) bird songs are hardwired into the brain. Other species, such as marsh wrens, learn by imitating what they hear. American robins share some whistles with neighbors, so they apparently learn song elements from one another. Baltimore orioles may learn their songs from their fathers and neighboring orioles during their first summer.

Birds really do sing loudest and with more energy and variety at dawn (or an hour or so before dawn in spring and early summer). Ornithologists don't know exactly why this is. It could be that they have a lot of energy after a good night's sleep or that in the dim light, their territorial competitors and prospective mates don't have much else to do besides listen. Or it could be that they have hopes that the singing might attract potential mates that may have landed after a night of migration.

GERALD D. TANG

SOARING THROUGH THE SKIES

Certainly, one of the most fascinating things about birds is their ability to glide through midair. Learn what enables them to take to the skies and why birds' wings can differ from species to species.

There is diversity in the shapes of bird wings, and the differences relate to how the birds use them. A northern bobwhite gets around mostly by walking, and only occasionally has to make a quick flight to scurry away from danger. Its wings are quite short and rounded, ideal for a rapid escape but not for sustained flight. On the other hand, a barn swallow spends most of the day in the air. Its wings are longer than its body and sharply pointed.

▶ BUILT TO GLIDE

Bird flight is a complex process dictated by wing structure and the air. Birds' wings are shaped to form an airfoil; when a bird moves forward through the air, the shape and curve of the wing cause the air to flow faster above the wing than below it. The faster air above lowers the pressure (drawing the bird upward) while the slower air below raises the pressure (pushing the bird upward). This force holding the bird up is called lift, and it requires that the bird be moving forward or facing into a fairly stiff wind.

RICK & NORA BOWERS/IMAGE FINDERS

Magnificent frigatebird

◀ **WING SMARTS**
The wings of birds that don't take to the air aren't useless. An ostrich dashing across the African plains sticks its stubby, fluffy wings out to the side to help balance during high-speed turns. Penguins use theirs as flippers to propel them in powerful, graceful swimming—in effect "flying" underwater.

When a bird isn't flying, it folds its wings neatly and tucks them against its body, out of the way. What's more, when the wings are closed, the feathers that are most important for flight are folded under the others, protecting them against wear and tear.

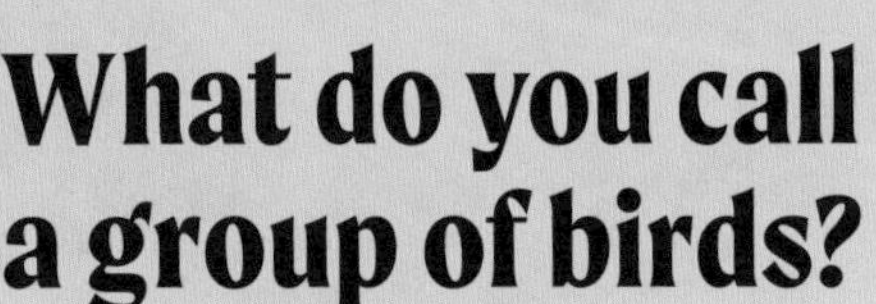

What do you call a group of birds?

Did you know that a group of red-eyed vireos is collectively known as a hangover? Or that a group of crows can be referred to as a hover, muster, parcel or parliament? Some terms are well known—such as flock or flight—but here are some others that may not be as familiar:

- A chain of bobolinks
- A gulp of cormorants
- A dole of doves
- A charm of finches
- A bevy of larks
- A tittering or tiding of magpies
- A stare or wisdom of owls
- A covey of ptarmigan
- A host or knot of sparrows
- A chattering or murmation of starlings
- A descent of woodpeckers
- A herd of wrens
- A marathon of roadrunners
- A brood or clutch of chicks
- A party, scold, or band of jays

Peregrine falcon

THE FASTEST BIRDS IN NORTH AMERICA

Being the fastest has its advantages for birds. In outwitting predators, raising a family or being the first to recognize a new source of food, being fast can boost a bird's chances of survival. Who wins the race in your yard?

◀ FASTEST SPEED

Peregrine falcons are the fastest on Earth. Not much time to get out of the way if you're the prey of a peregrine falcon—the superbly aerodynamic bird can reach almost 250 mph when it tucks its wings and goes into a headfirst dive. That's by far the fastest speed of any animal on Earth.

Bold, curious chickadees will be the first to eat from your hand. A handful of nuts makes a great bribe to coax birds into eating out of your hand; chickadees are usually the fastest to check out the new "feeder," followed by their titmice cousins. Nuthatches, especially the tiny red-breasted, are also relatively easy to hand-tame.

PICTURE PRESS RM/GETTY IMAGES

▼ FASTEST BUG-CATCHERS

Swallows, swifts and purple martins are the fastest bug-catchers. Tirelessly coursing the air at about 30 mph, these incredible insect eaters gulp down anything and everything, from tiny gnats to big dragonflies and butterflies. Each species has its preferred altitude: Tree swallows usually stay within 40 feet of the ground, while purple martins patrol as high as 500 feet.

Robins are the quickest to start singing. Each bird species begins singing when the light intensity reaches a certain point, and American robins respond to a much lower level of light than others—they'll start singing an hour or two before dawn. Even the glow of sodium-vapor streetlights may set robins singing.

Tree swallow

Mourning dove

▲ FASTEST NEST BUILDERS

Mourning doves race to finish their nests. Most birds spend several days to two weeks getting their home right, but a pair of mourning doves can throw together a loose platform of sticks in just a few hours. Why the hurry? Mourning doves may raise as many as six broods in a single year, each one in a new nest.

LEFT: STEVE BYLAND; RIGHT: ROLF NUSSBAUMER

Blackpoll warbler

Several species are ready to run right after birth. Caring for youngsters usually requires at least 10 days in the nest and several days after they leave or "fledge." But baby killdeer, quail, grouse, wild turkeys and sandpipers of all sorts are precocious, fuzzy-feathered and able to run as soon as they say "hello" to the world.

◂ FASTEST MIGRATOR

Blackpoll warblers travel the fastest during migration. Fall migration for the blackpoll warbler is a super marathon combined with a binge of weight gain and loss. Their epic trip from northern Canada to South America includes 2,000 miles across the open water of the Atlantic Ocean. They may fly that stretch nonstop, for more than 80 hours!

▶ FASTEST TO HATCH

House wrens are speediest to hatch. Most common backyard birds' eggs hatch in 11 to 14 days—but on occasion, house wren eggs may hatch in only nine days, although 12 days is more typical. You'll know the moment, however, because the babies begin cheeping.

Red-breasted mergansers zoom in horizontal flight. Good luck focusing those binoculars on them. This large duck has the fastest horizontal flight among birds, easily reaching 70 mph. Among common backyard birds, the prize goes to the mourning dove, which typically rockets along at about 40 mph. As a comparison, most birds fly at about 25 mph.

STEVE AND DAVE MASLOWSKI

House wrens

◀ FASTEST WINGBEAT

Hummingbirds have the fastest wingbeat. The smaller the hummingbird, the faster its little wings go. The ruby-throated hummingbird beats about 50 times a second. The bee hummingbird of Cuba, the smallest bird on Earth at only 2 inches from bill tip to tail tip, buzzes along at 80 beats per second.

We'd have to eat 300 cheeseburgers a day to keep up with hummingbirds' metabolisms. Hummers have one of the fastest metabolisms in the animal kingdom, but it slows down when the bird isn't flying. That's why hummingbirds spend most of their waking hours perched and resting—although you'd never guess it from looking at your feeders.

▼ QUICKEST SPRINTERS

Greater roadrunners are speedy sprinters. In North America, our quickest land bird is the greater roadrunner. Its usual pace is 20 mph, and it can reach about 26 mph in top gear. Still, it's a slowpoke compared to the ostrich, which can sprint at 50 mph.

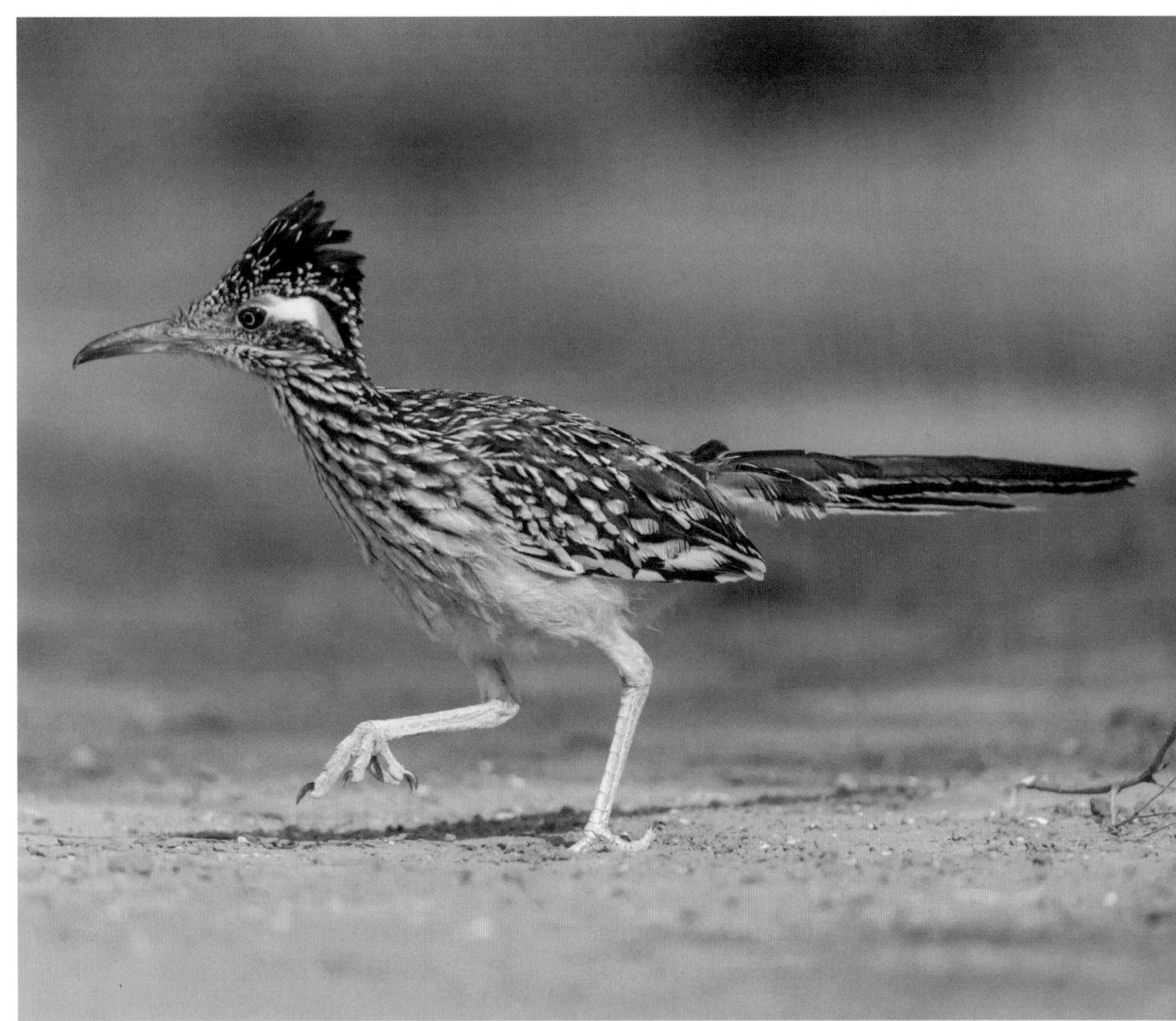

DENNIS W DONOHUE/SHUTTERSTOCK

WHAT'S HATCHING?

Explore how egg color, size and incubation vary from species to species.

Cranes lay two relatively small eggs that are pale brown and marked with reddish brown blotches for camouflage. Both parents attend the nest and spend about a month taking turns incubating the eggs, but this is just a small fraction of their parental duties. They spend the next nine months looking after the young until they become independent.

▶ BLUE JAYS

These fliers remove sharp eggshell fragments to protect their newly hatched brood from harm. This action also prevents both microbial infestations and pungent-smelling cues that might alert nest predators about the location of the clutch. In this jay's family, only the female incubates the eggs, but both parents work to provision the hungry chicks upon hatching.

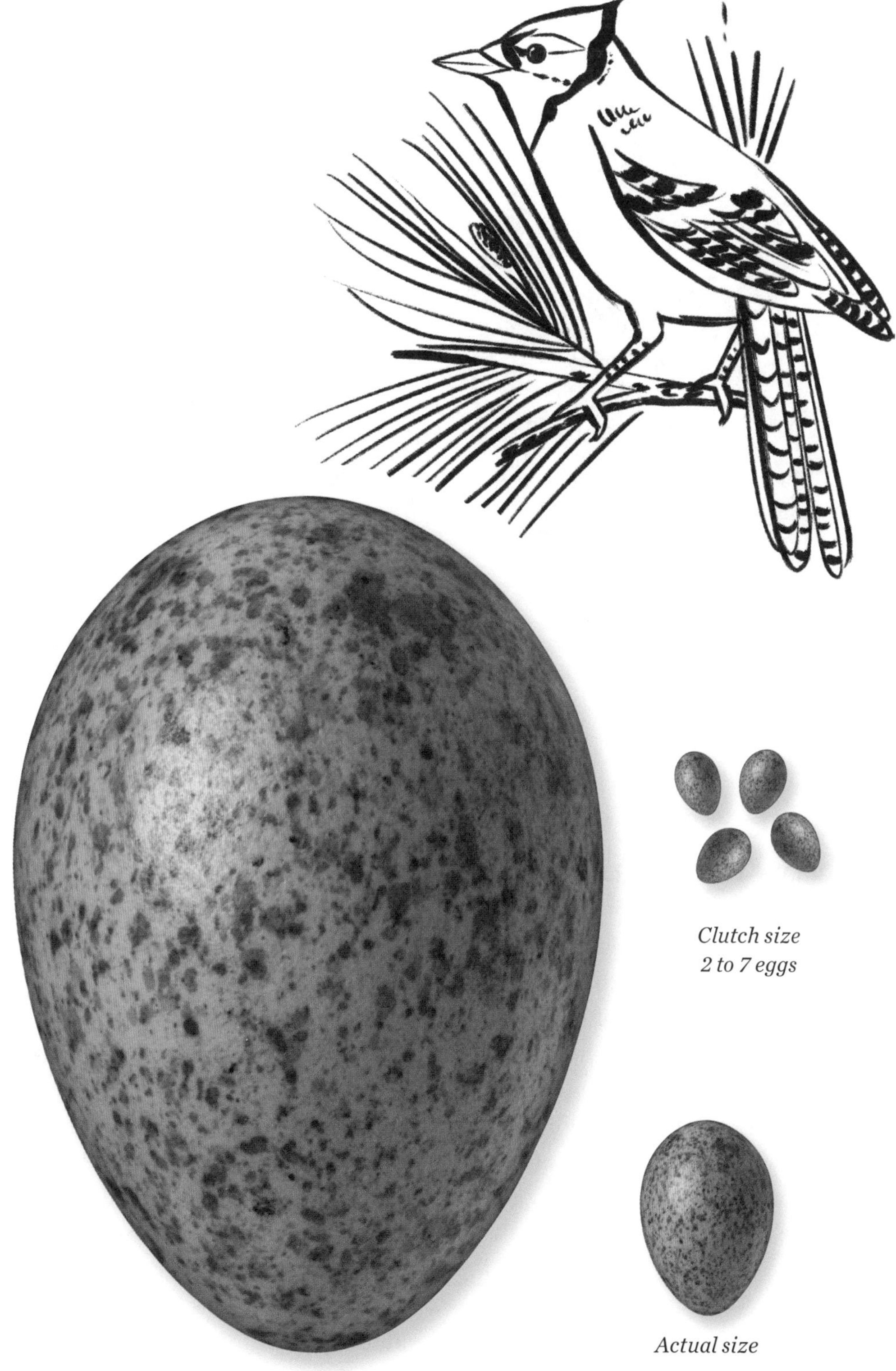

Clutch size
2 to 7 eggs

Actual size

JOHN WEINSTEIN, FIELD MUSEUM

Clutch size 4 to 5 eggs

Actual size

▲ YELLOW WARBLERS

They are popular targets of brood parasitic brown-headed cowbirds. When both species' eggs are present in a nest, the warbler eggs often fail to hatch or the chicks might not make it to fledging. When cowbirds are near the nest, yellow warblers emit alarm calls and the female may sit on the nest with wings spread out to keep other birds at bay.

Birders rarely glimpse the eggs of black-capped chickadees because those fliers prefer to breed in old woodpecker holes or in holes of rotting stumps. There is a trade-off, though. Because woodpecker holes are safer than artificial nest boxes, competition with other cavity-nesting birds for the holes is also much fiercer.

The spotless bright blue-green eggs in the American robin's nest are a sign that spring has arrived in North America. Many eggs don't make it to hatching because of the diverse predators—including squirrels, snakes and crows—that easily rob the robin clutch. In response to adversity, robins quickly build their nests again, but the later clutches might contain fewer eggs.

▼ CEDAR WAXWINGS
Erratic in their distribution and where they breed, cedar waxwings time their egg laying with late-ripening fruit. The waxwing egg is a balance of a pale bluish gray and a suite of darker, delicate spotting patterns. With a tight pair bond, both parents build the nest, incubate the eggs and, once the eggs hatch, feed the nestlings a mostly fruit diet.

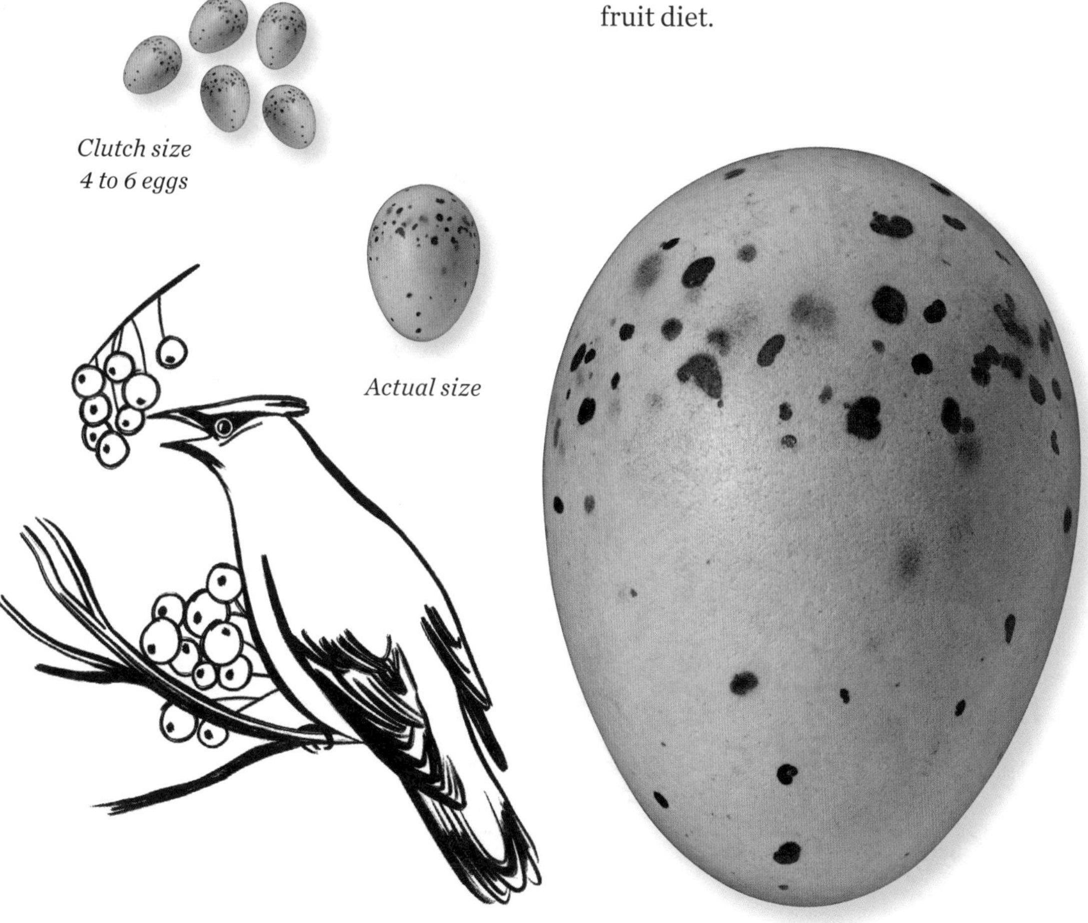

JOHN WEINSTEIN, FIELD MUSEUM

▼ CARDINALS

The beige base color and brown spots of the cardinal's egg contrast with the bright red plumage of the male parent. The female is responsible for incubating the eggs; she also builds the delicate nest, constructing the base by crushing twigs with her powerful beak. All the while, she's followed and fed by the male as part of his nuptial feedings.

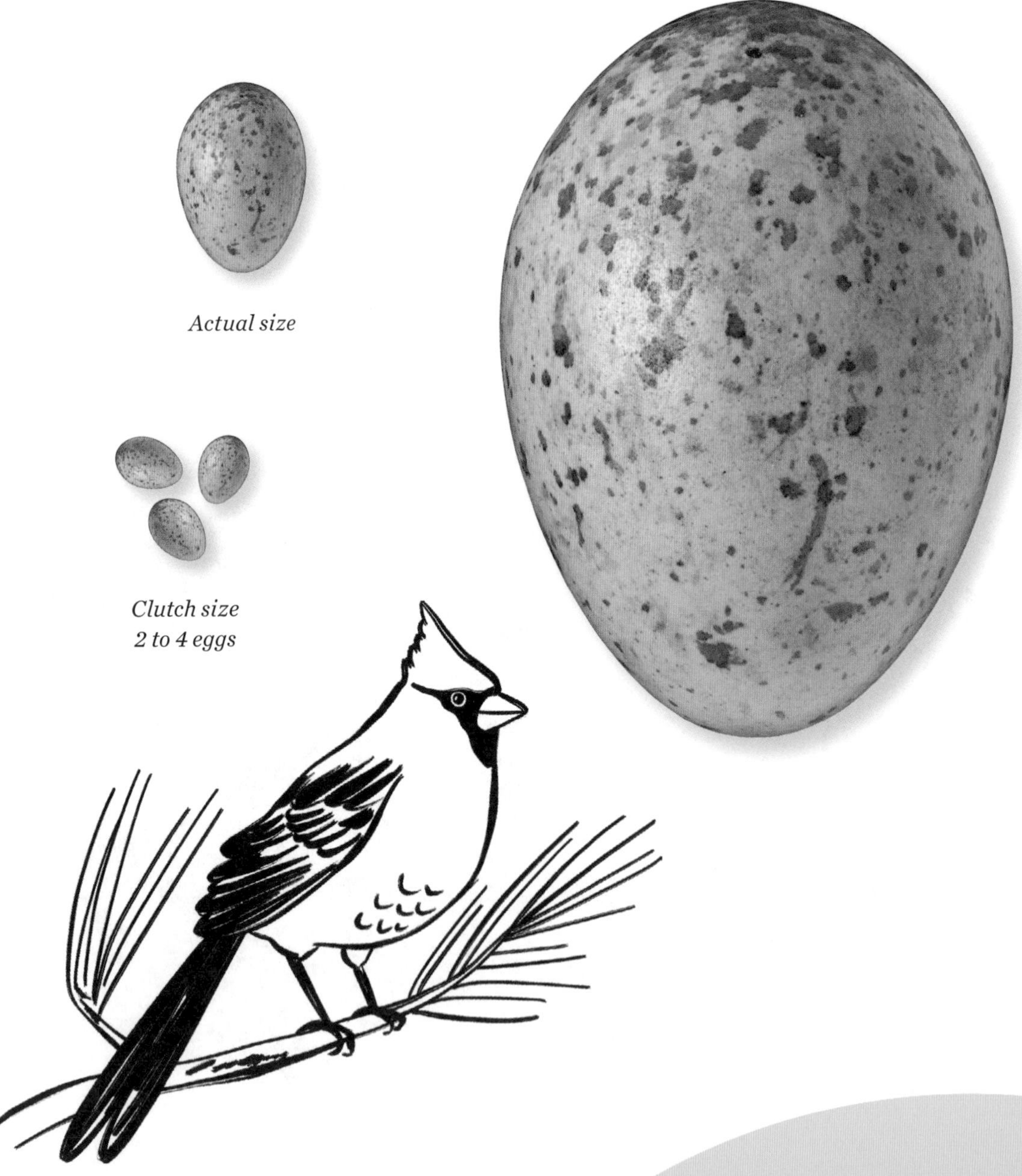

Actual size

Clutch size
2 to 4 eggs

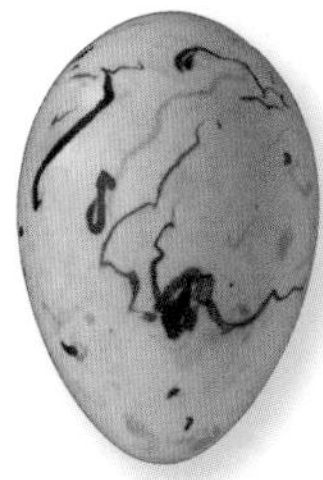

Actual size

Clutch size
3 to 7 eggs

▶ ORIOLES

The pale gray-blue oriole egg is covered with sparsely distributed lines and squiggles that marble the egg. Occasionally, a nest may be attended by two birds that look like females. But usually one of them is actually a young male breeding for his first time, still displaying more cryptic plumage.

It takes an osprey five weeks or so to complete the incubation period for its dark blotch-covered eggs. Older birds often pair with previous partners, reusing and improving the preceding year's nest to build an even bulkier—and presumably safer—site for incubating the eggs.

JOHN WEINSTEIN, FIELD MUSEUM

"The reason birds can fly and we can't is simply because they have perfect faith, for to have faith is to have wings."

—J.M. BARRIE

Tufted titmouse

Cedar waxwings

DATING & MATING

When it comes to courtship, birds pull out all the stops, using elaborate displays to attract a potential mate and outdo the competition. Here are some courtly behaviors to look for in spring.

◀ SHARING A BITE

Cedar waxwings love berries, so when a male wants to express interest in a female, he side-hops next to her and offers the fruit. If she accepts it, she hops back and forth, then returns it to him. This continues until the berry is eaten.

Sharp-tailed grouses "perform" in an "arena" to find a mate. This grouse species uses a lek—a mating arena of sorts—where males perform to attract females. Male sharp-tailed grouse stick their pointed tails up, aim their wings down and inflate purple air sacs along their necks. Then they quickly shake and vibrate their entire bodies while cooing out. Females visit the lek during these displays and select a male to breed with.

JOHANN SCHUMACHER DESIGN

▲ FALLING IN LOVE

Bald eagles free-fall for love. Mated partners lock talons in midflight and then spiral in a free-fall dive known as cartwheeling. Red-tailed and other hawks will cartwheel in courtship, too. Eagles often mate for life, and pairs will return to the same nests year after year. Male bald eagles help with nest construction and raising the eaglets.

Ruffed grouse perform alone. Perched on a downed log, the male, starting slowly at first but quickly accelerating, flaps his cupped wings, creating a deep whooshing that sounds like a tractor starting up on a cold morning. This short burst of chest drumming reverberates through the forest, which helps females find potential mates.

Great horned owls sing together, too. Owls are early nesters; listen for their characteristic hoots on cold, crisp winter nights. Female great horned owls are bigger than males, but males have larger voice boxes. When you hear them calling back and forth, try to pick up the male's deeper voice and the female's corresponding higher pitched hoots. Males assist throughout the entire nesting season and will bring food to the nest for the female and young.

Song sparrows sing a variety of songs in courtship. Song sparrow males can sing as many as 20 different songs while defending territories and courting females. Some studies indicate that a female song sparrow chooses a mate based in part on his ability to learn new songs.

The 6 Love Languages of Birds

Birds exhibit all sorts of behaviors as part of their courtship rituals.

SINGING
Vocalizations of various lengths and intricacies.

DANCING
Rhythmic movements, such as wing flapping, head bobbing, and moving up and down.

POSTURING
Positions designed to show off a bird's size and feathers.

ALLOPREENING
One bird cleans another's feathers with its beak.

BUILDING
Constructing (and sometimes decorating) a nest to catch the attention of a potential mate.

FEEDING
One bird feeds food to another using its beak.

Northern cardinal

MARIE READ

◀ DRAWN TO SONG
Northern cardinals sing a duet. Male cardinals have bright red plumage that impresses females, but courting for this species goes deeper than surface attraction. Females sing along with the males during courtship. Experts believe the duet strengthens the bond. In your backyard, listen for pure, repetitive whistling from cardinal pairs. Females sometimes call while on the nest; males bring food to the females to ensure nesting success.

Great blue herons engage in a variety of behaviors during courtship, and many of them revolve around building a nest. This includes sweet little gestures like exchanging twigs. To construct the big, bulky nest, the male does most of the gathering, picking up sticks from the ground or from unguarded nests. The female does most of the work of putting the nest material in place.

Red-shouldered hawks

Field Notes

A Lucky Pair

Whenever I spend an early morning walking through my local park, I usually see a hawk soaring past, looking for something to eat. This particular morning a male and a female red-shouldered hawk were flying around, and they both landed on a nearby tree. I just happened to have my camera with me, and was thrilled I could get this picture.

—Alice Beaman, Brazil, Indiana

▶ MARKING THEIR TERRITORY

House wrens are prolific backyard singers. A male's singing is mostly a territorial claim. To find mates, males must choose good nest sites—which are often close to people, so you're likely to hear them. They use natural cavities, but they also like nest boxes. Males construct partial nests in multiple sites, and the females select from the offerings. When a female finds a suitable site, she mates with the owner.

ALICE BEAMAN

Common terns go fishing for a mate. To advertise his territory, a male tern flies over the colony with a fish. Courtship begins when a female follows and the male gives her his catch. After more behaviors, such as posturing and strutting, the male continues to feed the female until she lays a clutch of eggs.

▼ MAKING MOVES

Sandhill cranes are elegant dancers. Experts do not completely understand the behavior, but it seems to play a role in bonding. Mated sandhill cranes also sing a unison call during courtship. Curiously, young birds also dance—believed to be an important part of their motor development.

Sandhill cranes

DANYU/SHUTTERSTOCK

Mute swans

▲ NECKS TOGETHER

Mute swans engage in preening, too. During the lengthy courtship process, the two swans stick close together and begin to quickly preen themselves. After several minutes, they synchronize their postures, like the swan pair here.

American avocets show off. During courtship, avocets engage in posturing. Before breeding, the male avocet dips his bill in water to preen himself. Afterward, the avocet pair intertwine their necks and cross their beaks.

Wood ducks

JOHN YINGER

Field Notes

Duck Hug

Several years ago, I decided to take my camera and go out to the lake, about 50 yards or so behind our house. I built a duck blind back there in hopes of capturing some good photos of the ducks and shorebirds in our area.

On this particular morning, I spotted six wood ducks flying into the water. Soon, a male and female pair swam off by themselves, so I kept a close watch on them. I noticed the female, flattening out her body and swimming circles around the male. He just ignored her, though. Then she started pecking at his neck, which finally seemed to get his attention. This went on for about 15 minutes, and I snapped this photo before they fluffed up their feathers and swam off.

This was definitely something I don't see every day at my blind, and I loved getting these good photos. It was a very exciting morning for me.

—John Yinger, Columbus, Ohio

SPECIAL SECTION

BRAINY BIRDS

When it comes to smart birds, we humans still have a lot to learn. Bird intelligence comes in many forms, and scientists are finding that many species exhibit a mental aptitude similar to that of marine mammals, apes and even humans. Take a look at the smartest bird species in America and get bragging rights for knowing about their brainy behavior.

Planning and Memorizing

Woodpeckers and jays hoard nuts for later feeding; the collecting and caching of food is an example of planning for the future. The birds' ability to find their hidden treasure later on demonstrates impressive long-term memory. Similarly, fruit eaters such as robins and cedar waxwings remember where specific trees are and when they will fruit. Hummingbirds recall which individual plants in their habitat are rich with nectar, and will return each year to those flowers, trees or bushes.

Blue jays

JANET WACHTER

Crows

Working Together

Smart birds work cooperatively and understand the concepts of mutual benefit and the greater good. Harris's hawks of the Southwest hunt in family packs similar to those of wolves or lions, working together to flush and ambush prey. Wild turkeys line up wing to wing and walk across fields. They know they can flush more insects in that formation than if they scattered or walked single file. Crows live in highly structured family groups comprising several generations. They readily team up to mob predators, knowing there is strength in numbers.

The smartest bird species are even wise enough to transcend species barriers. Chickadees and nuthatches, for example, have been observed responding to each other's predator warning calls, in a kind of predator-alert symbiosis.

RHEA HAYES

Common robin

Recognizing Faces

Many birds bravely defend their nests, attacking potential predators to drive them away, but this defensive behavior is typically indiscriminate. Any perceived threat is mobbed or dive-bombed. Yet a recent study of northern mockingbirds found that they not only recognize individuals of a potentially dangerous species, but they also remember an individual's past behavior and single him or her out for attack.

Researchers determined this by asking a series of people to approach a mockingbird nest. One particular person approached the nest several times. The birds learned to recognize this individual and could actually pick him out of a crowd. They marked him as a threat and preemptively attacked him while ignoring others who randomly walked by the nest.

As it happens, this behavior has been reported anecdotally in other species as well, including robins. Further research could well reveal that still other kinds of birds have this ability to recognize not just a threatening species but a particular human or other potential predator—undeniably a promising sign of sophisticated intelligence.

Mimics

Speaking of mockingbirds, they're astonishing in their ability to learn and mimic foreign noises. They get their name, of course, from the ease with which they can deliver the songs of shrikes, blackbirds, orioles, killdeer, jays, hawks and even frogs. Other smart birds are almost as versatile.

Steller's jays mimic many wild birds, as well as chickens, squirrels, cats and dogs. Blue jays expertly imitate red-shouldered hawks. European starlings (which, despite their name, are widespread in North America) learn and repeat the songs of eastern wood pewee, killdeer, meadowlarks and many others. They even mimic cellphone ring tones and other urban noises. In captivity, the exceptionally intelligent raven has been taught to mimic human words. Move over, Polly!

Mockingbird

STEVEN BIEGLER

Solving Problems

Some smart birds are savvy enough to use trial and error to adapt to new situations. Bald eagles have been seen swimming across the surface of the water, dragging prey behind them, after attempts at holding on to the prize while in flight proved ineffectual. They'll also crack ice with their strong beaks. Then they jump up and down on it, breaking through to expose open water for fishing.

And we know that the smartest bird species understand cause and effect. Gulls drop mollusks and crustaceans from high in the air, letting them crash on the rocks to crack their hard shells. Ravens often follow the sounds of hunters' gunshots. They have learned that such noises mean the possibility of scavenging the remains of the game after field dressing.

Bald eagle

Green heron

Using Tools

Tool use was once believed to be exclusive to humans—one of the things that set us apart from all other species. But study after study has shown that many other species use tools to survive. We take for granted that nest-building birds use twigs, plant fibers, hair, spiderwebs, lichen, mud and even plastic to construct nests—which shows smart tool use. Other, even more astounding examples have come to light, though, showing how much smarter birds are than previously thought.

Predatory shrikes, lacking the strong talons of raptors to grip their prey while feeding, use thorns or even barbed wire to impale their victims for easier eating. Gila woodpeckers use bits of bark for scooping up honey to bring back to their young. Green herons have been observed fishing with bits of bread that people have tossed out for ducks. They use the bait to lure small fish to the surface, where they are easily caught.

One of the oldest and most whimsical stories of a bird aptly using a tool is the Aesop fable "The Crow and the Pitcher." In this tale, the crow drops pebbles into a pitcher of water, thereby raising the level of the liquid so it can take a drink. Animal behaviorists have confirmed that this trick wouldn't be beyond the capacity of an intelligent crow.

LEFT: JUSTIN ROSS; RIGHT: ELIZABETH MARTINE

7 SECRETS FOR SHOOING AWAY BULLY BIRDS

No meanies allowed! Here's how to free up backyard feeders for your favorite songbirds.

1 **Add a unique** new feeder to your yard. An upside-down thistle feeder allows smaller birds, such as American goldfinches, a place to eat while keeping larger bully birds away.

2 **Switch your seed** offerings. Some backyard birders say grackles don't like safflower seeds, so if you have a problem with them, adjust your food offerings. A lot of nuisance birds tend to leave nyjer (thistle) alone, too.

3 ▶ **LET BLUE JAYS HAVE THEIR OWN DOMAIN.** These birds are exceptionally smart, so it's not easy to outwit them with fancy jay-proof feeders. Your best bet for dealing with these beauties is to give them space and a feeder of their own—serve peanuts in a feeder or put sunflower seeds in a large hopper feeder in an isolated area.

Blue jay and cardinal

European starlings

DANNY BROWN

4 Adjust feeders to discourage grackles. Removing feeder perches should get rid of them; like many large birds, grackles can't cling to feeders to eat.

5 ◀ GET CREATIVE TO GET RID OF EUROPEAN STARLINGS. These boisterous birds love suet, and it's not uncommon for them to gobble up an entire suet cake in a day. Look for starling-proof feeders (food is accessible only from the bottom) or set up a suet feeder under a squirrel baffle.

6 ▶ TRY A TRICK WITH A TRAY

It's actually quite simple to stop blackbirds, pigeons and crows from bombarding your feeder. Just install a tray right underneath the feeder. It will catch any seed cast aside by songbirds and keep it off the ground.

7 Give weighted perches a whirl. If installing a tray doesn't fix the problem with blackbirds, pigeons or crows, try feeders with weighted perches. When a large bird or squirrel lands on the perch, a cover drops over the food.

Backyard Hacks

Our community of bird watchers share secrets for dealing with bully birds.

I keep aggressive hummingbirds to a minimum by placing multiple feeders in my front yard and a few in the back. Bullies can't be in two places at once, so the others get a chance to sip nectar too!

—Rebecca McLaughlin,
Flatwoods, Kentucky

Rock pigeons mobbed my feeders, so I bought green vinyl-coated wire mesh with 2-by-3-inch holes to surround the trays. Small songbirds get in, but pigeons can't!

—Andrew Rivinus,
Canby, Oregon

Upside-down suet feeders mostly attract nuthatches and woodpeckers, not bullies.

—Jennifer Broadstreet Hess,
Marion, Kansas

My favorite bird feeder has customizable perches and a large slippery dome. Heavier birds are too big for the feeder, and squirrels slide right off!

—Pat Brown,
Springfield, Virginia

We try to accommodate all of the birds, but it seems that in different circumstances any bird can be a bully! My mourning doves are bullies of the tray feeder. And I've even seen a titmouse chase Carolina wrens from the mealworms.

—Boni Trombetta,
West Chester, Pennsylvania

I call blue jays "beautiful bullies" because they, along with common grackles and starlings, can empty a peanut feeder in less than an hour. I use a cage around one peanut feeder to allow only smaller birds to feed. The jays get their own cage-free peanut feeder.

—Deanna Frautschi,
Bloomington, Illinois

Starlings, grackles, blue jays and the odd magpie come to my feeders and also stop for water. Instead of discouraging them, I spread several feeders full of different types of seed around the backyard.

—Ken Orich,
Lethbridge, Alberta

Eastern bluebird

"Birds! Birds!
Ye are beautiful
things, With your
earth-treading
feet and your
cloud-cleaving
wings!"

—ELIZA COOK

BILL LEAMAN

AROUND THE WORLD AND BACK AGAIN

Whether flying north to south or zigzagging between oceans, migrating birds have spectacular habits, flight patterns and ways of getting to where they need to go. Here are a few morsels to know about migration.

The species of birds you see during spring migration depends on the month of the year and your location. No matter where you are, the phenomenon lasts for months. Along the southern border it starts in January, while in the far North you might not see movement until March or even later.

▶ HEAD STARTS

Some early spring migrators make lengthy trips. Purple martins spend the first part of winter in South America but start their trek early, with advance scouts reaching Florida and Texas by the middle of January. In the far West, rufous and Allen's hummingbirds that have wintered in Mexico move north up the California coast as soon as early February.

Purple martin

Before heading south in fall, a bird may molt, or replace, its feathers over several weeks, so it travels in fresh plumage. It's likely to gorge itself on bugs or berries to build up stores of fat that serve as fuel on long flights.

▶ ROBIN BEHAVIOR

Some American robins fly from Canada to Florida in fall, but others in mild climates stay in the same place all year. An individual robin might even go south one year but remain up north the next.

◀ FLIGHT PATTERNS

Although we think of birds as flying north in spring and south in fall, they don't all fit that assumption. Some hummingbirds in the Southwest and Mexico begin their "spring" flight in January, and certain species travel east and west rather than north and south.

DAWN WEISS

American robin

▶ **WARBLER SEASON**
Warblers return in April or May. Because they feed mainly on insects, they travel when they can rely on warm temperatures. Their peak flight is in April in the southern states and in May farther north. On the right spring morning at favored spots in the eastern states, it's possible to catch sight of 20 or more species of warblers.

An oriole that nests in your area could make its way to Central America, the Caribbean or even South America in the fall. And in spring, the same oriole might return to your yard. Though it seems far-fetched, it's not all that unique—most migrants match this feat.

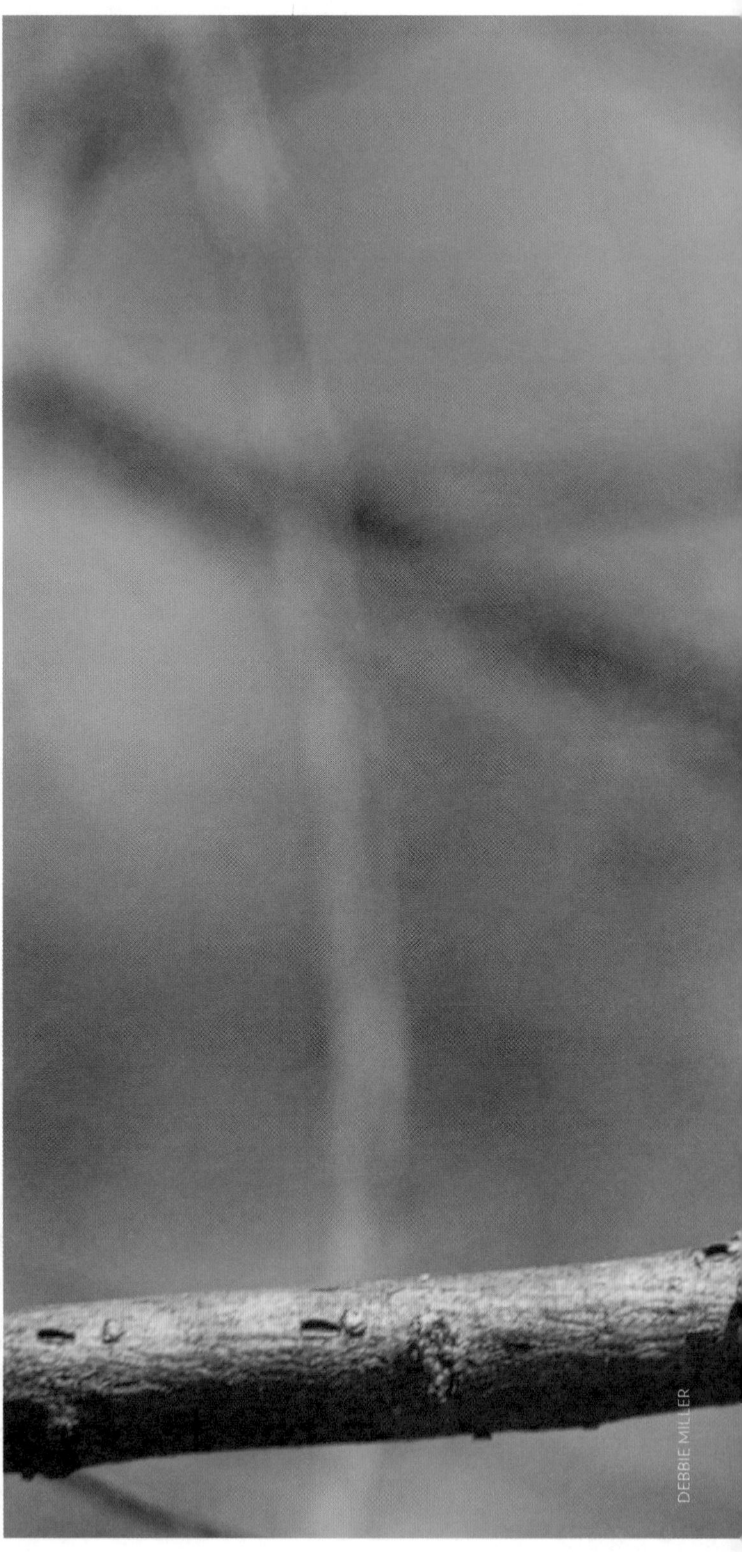

DEBBIE MILLER

Prothonotary warbler

Sandhill crane

Field Notes

Sandhill cranes

These birds fly through Kentucky every year during migration. They land on my sister's farm, where I watch their graceful movements and playful antics around the cornfield. They're truly beautiful.

—Liz Tabb
Elizabethtown, Kentucky

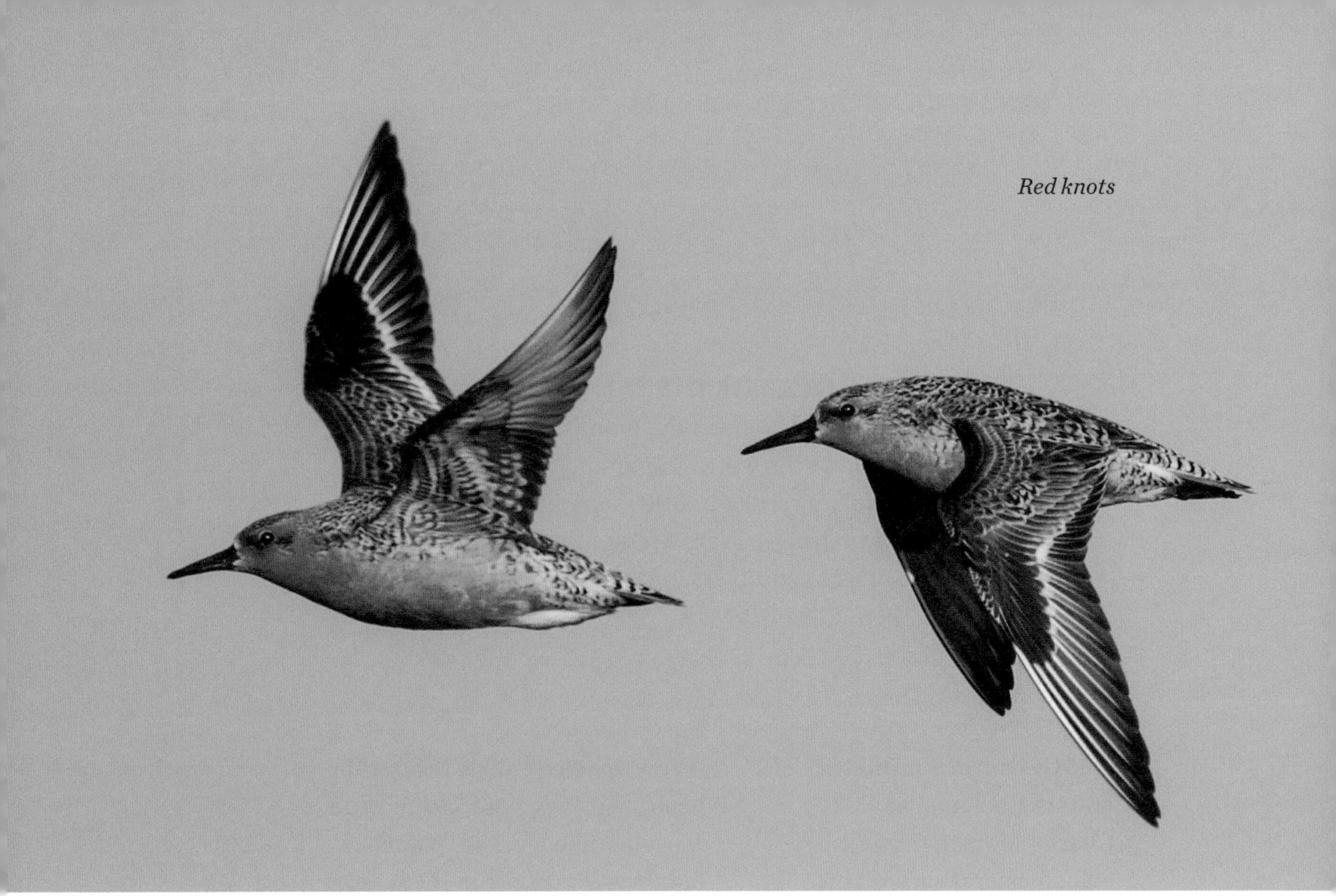

Red knots

▲ SOARING TO THE NEXT MEAL

Red knots are professionals at eating on the go—with a highly specialized migration strategy. The annual journey of this shorebird species coincides with the spring breeding of horseshoe crabs on the East Coast, and thousands of red knots take full advantage of the May buffet. Red knots are found worldwide, but among those that migrate through eastern North America, up to 90 percent may be present on the beaches of Delaware Bay at once.

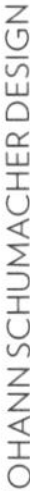

Ruby-throated hummingbirds fly straight over the Gulf of Mexico. It takes ruby throats about 18 hours to make the journey, a lot faster than if they had taken a detour along the coast. Before they take off on their solitary flights, they fuel up and put on weight, and if they get tired en route, they sometimes rest on boats.

JOHANN SCHUMACHER DESIGN

▶ GOING THE DISTANCE

If bird migrations were marathons, the arctic tern would be the world champion marathoner. They travel upward of 25,000 miles annually on their epic journeys. From Arctic summers in the North to Antarctic summers in the South, their odysseys take them to every ocean.

A 17th-century minister and scientist named Charles Morton tried to explain migration with his odd theory that birds went to the moon and back, flying 125 mph to reach their out-of-this-world destination in 60 days.

A few species trickle in after the peak of spring migration concludes. Most members of the flycatcher family show up late in the season, because they feed on insects caught in midair and the weather has to be warm before bugs start flying around. That situation also could explain the late arrival of the common nighthawk, another aerial insect-eater.

ATTILA JANDI/SHUTTERSTOCK

Arctic tern

INSIDER'S GUIDE

THE ULTIMATE GUIDE TO CHOOSING AND MAINTAINING A BIRD FEEDER

There are many types of feeders available for your feathered friends. Discover them and get tips for drawing birds right to them. Also, take our hacks for cleaning and maintaining feeders, and follow the do's and don'ts for making your own seed.

The Right Feeder Makes All the Difference

A quick flyover of all the different types of bird feeders you can buy.

Thistle feeder. Often tube-shaped, thistle feeders are specially made to hold thistle (nyjer) seed, which goldfinches love. Some thistle feeders are a simple mesh bag, while others are sturdier. You can even get some that are several feet long, holding dozens of goldfinches at a time.

Tray feeder. These types of feeders can either hang or sit atop legs on the ground. In both cases they are completely open, so birds have a big space to land and eat. Tray feeders are often favored by larger birds like mourning doves and ground-feeders like juncos. Some people who love squirrels even put out their corncobs on tray feeders.

▶ **TUBE FEEDER**
If it's not a thistle feeder, other tube feeders have larger holes for seed like sunflowers and safflowers. Often good squirrel deterrents, look for tube feeders with a weighted contraption that closes off seed access when larger birds or squirrels land.

American goldfinches

Oriole

◀ **FRUIT FEEDER**

You can find a handful of other feeders on the market, including those that hold jelly or fruit such as grapes, oranges and apples. These are great feeders to experiment with, especially in spring and fall, when you'll see the most migrants.

Sugar-water feeder. This feeder is pretty self-explanatory. You can find it in a few standard shapes, and it's for those glorious little fliers we call hummingbirds. Keep in mind that a second sugar-water feeder (usually in an orange color) will attract orioles and other birds.

Suet feeder. There are more than a half-dozen suet feeders on the market, including the classic cage design and one with the cage attached to a vertical wooden platform, which gives woodpeckers a better way to perch with their tails.

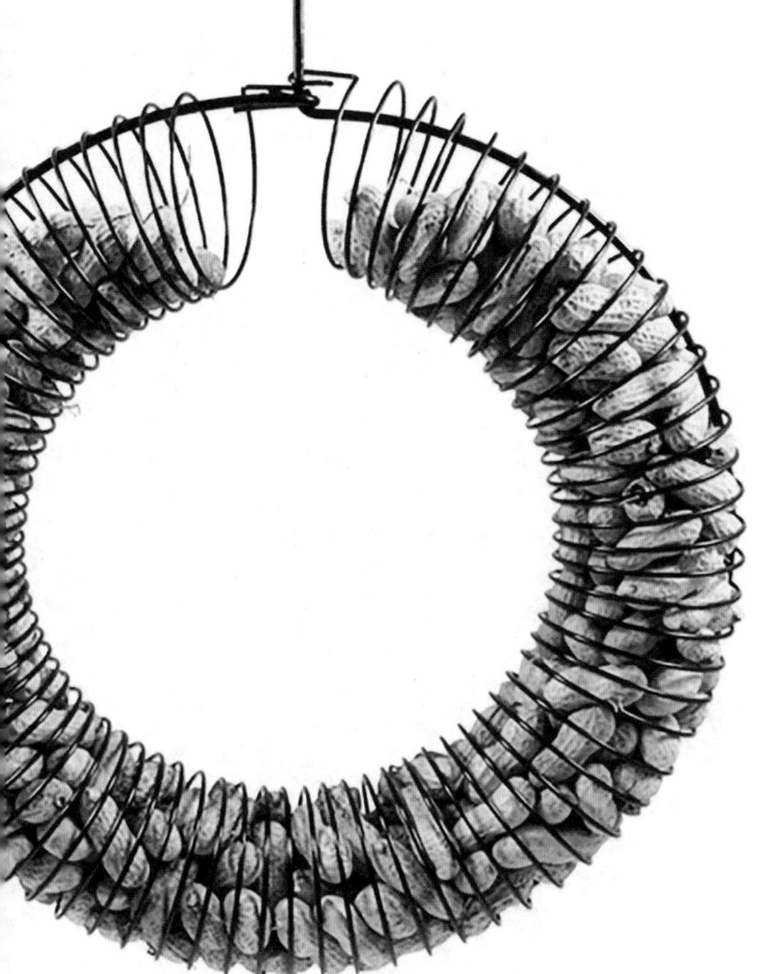

Log feeder. You can't get thriftier than taking an old log and drilling holes in the side. These holes are perfect for suet or straight peanut butter. Plus, the log gives woodpeckers and other birds a handy built-in perch.

Hopper feeder. The classic hopper usually has four sides, and it's common to find in the shape of a house or a barn. Sometimes you can even find options with suet feeders on either end. While it typically doesn't deter squirrels, it does offer a surefire way to offer black oil sunflower seeds to birds of all sizes.

▲ PEANUT FEEDER
It's usually shaped like a tube, but you can also find peanut feeders in wreath shapes. These feeders have a spiral design, so the birds (and sometimes squirrels) have to work to get the peanuts out.

Ruby-throated hummingbird

Bring in the Birds

Follow these expert tips and you'll be hosting a feeding frenzy.

◀ **SKIP THE RED DYE**
Experts agree that red dye in hummingbird food is not only unnecessary, it could actually harm hummingbirds. The safest, most inexpensive way to provide hummingbird food (aside from adding native plants) is making your own: Stir 4 parts water with 1 part pure cane sugar. Bring to a boil, cool completely and fill your feeders.

Avoid grease. In your quest to discourage squirrels from dining at your feeders, steer clear of grease or oil on hooks, poles or posts. Any oily substance can be harmful, or even fatal, to birds if they get it on their precious feathers.

Deter unwanted guests. It's a challenge to keep squirrels from gobbling up bird seed. Enter baffles. You'll find a variety of these deterring devices, from simple to elaborate, on the market. Because squirrels are crafty little critters, you might need to try several to find one that baffles your marauders.

Go beyond seed. Adding variety to the menu attracts more kinds of birds. Black oil sunflower, thistle (Nyjer) seed and white millet are three of the staples. Add oranges and apples to attract orioles and catbirds, suet to lure woodpeckers and peanuts to entice titmice, chickadees and nuthatches.

Remember: location, location, location. Windows reflect outdoor scenery, so they pose a real danger to birds. If window strikes are a problem at your house, do whatever you can to reduce them. Hawk silhouettes on the glass may help, but we suggest using a product from American Bird Conservancy called BirdTape. It breaks up light and reflections so birds don't try to fly through.

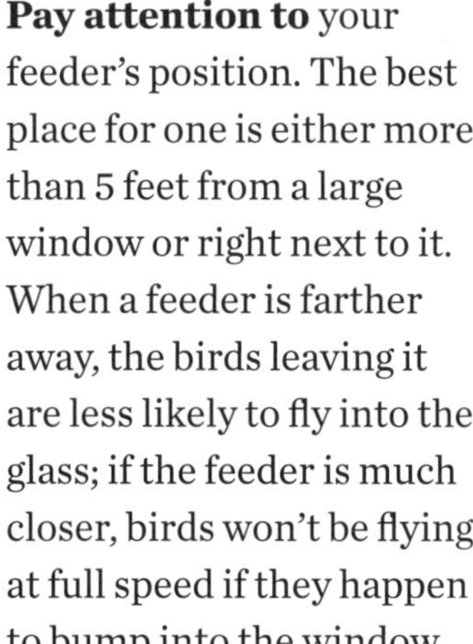

Pay attention to your feeder's position. The best place for one is either more than 5 feet from a large window or right next to it. When a feeder is farther away, the birds leaving it are less likely to fly into the glass; if the feeder is much closer, birds won't be flying at full speed if they happen to bump into the window.

Curious cat

◀ DON'T LET THE CAT OUT

When you put bird feeders and wandering cats together, it's a recipe for disaster. Keeping cats indoors is better for native wildlife and for the cats, too. If cats roam your neighborhood, either don't put out feeders or be sure to position them away from spots where the cats might lurk in ambush.

Share the joy. One of the easiest ways to bring happiness to people's lives is to share your love of birds. Show your backyard birds to guests—or better yet, help your friends and family with their own setup. A feeder and a bag of seed is a wonderful gift that keeps on giving for years.

Enjoy your visitors! Keeping feeders clean and full may feel like a big chore at times, so make sure to reward yourself by actually watching the birds. Their behaviors are endlessly varied, and you'll learn new things almost every day.

▲ **OFFER WATER YEAR-ROUND**
Many songbirds stop over at feeders, but if you want to attract types that don't eat seeds—such as warblers, vireos or thrushes—plan on making water a part of your feeding routine. The most natural location for a birdbath is on the ground. Make sure the basin isn't too deep; if your birdbath is more than 2 inches deep, add a layer of pea gravel to the bottom.

Maintenance Tips

It's easy to keep your feeders clean—and your seed fresh—with these useful tidbits.

Good storage is essential. You could even say that the seed you use is only as good as your storage method. Store your seeds in a sealed container, away from mice, squirrels and other critters. This will keep your area tidy and birds healthy.

▶ MORE IS BETTER
Crowded spaces lead to messy surroundings, so if you have a single feeder constantly being mobbed by visitors, then maybe it's time to put out another one. This will alleviate the high traffic, and it'll help keep your feeding space cleaner longer.

Keep seed dry. Birds will avoid food that has been out in the rain, and even when it dries, the food is usually moldy—a potential hazard. If you can, set your feeders up under a protected area, away from the rain and damp. If this isn't an option, then be sure to clean them out after the rain.

Keep feeders clean. A good rule of thumb is to clean your feeders at least once with every new season. (An exception is hummingbird feeders, which should be cleaned every week or two during the height of the season.) Scrub with a mixture of 10 parts water to 1 part bleach.

RICHARD DAY/DAYBREAK IMAGERY

American goldfinches

Homemade seed wreath

DIY Birdseed Do's & Don'ts

Secrets for saving money by making your own DIY birdseed mix.

DO

◀ EXPERIMENT WITH FUN SHAPES.
Combine your homemade seed mix with unflavored gelatin and water, spread it on a cookie sheet and let it chill. Then, form it into shapes like wreaths, stars, hearts or whatever cookie cutters you've got on hand.

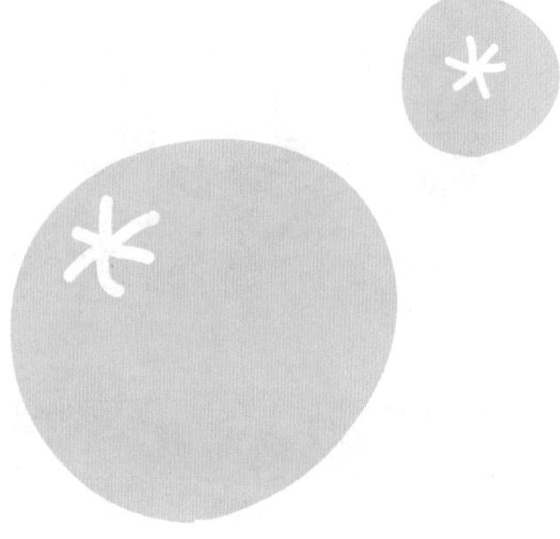

DON'T

Use messy seed. There are certain types of seed that are messier than others. Red millet, for example, often gets tossed to the ground by common songbirds. Even though sparrows, doves and cardinals eat millet, it might be a good idea to skip it.

DO

Offer birds their favorite foods. Watch birds at your feeders and take note of what they're eating or tossing to the ground, then experiment with different blends. For example, you can try adding dried cranberries to see if you attract a new species.

MARK DERSE

3 Check out as usual! The cashier will weigh and price your items.
HOW TO SHOP IN Bulk
1 Fill a container or bag with the amount you want.
2 Write the PLU number on the twist tie or label.
3 Check out as usual! The cashier will weigh and price your items.
HOW TO SHOP IN Bulk

DO

◀ **BUY SUPPLIES IN BULK.**
If you know you're going to use a lot of sunflower or safflower seeds while creating your homemade concoctions, it's best to buy your supplies in mass quantities. Membership big-box stores are great places to stock up and get a decent deal.

DON'T

Attract unwanted visitors. Inexpensive store-bought seed blends can occasionally attract pesky visitors. These seed blends might contain red millet (white proso millet is a better option), wheat or other grain products that are typically used as filler. Avoid those things when creating your own birdseed mix and stick with only quality seeds and foods.

WOODKERN/GETTY IMAGES

Reader-Tested Recipes

Birds & Blooms experts share their no-fail mixes.

For a super simple seed combo, just incorporate black oil sunflower seed with cracked corn and plenty of peanuts.

—Tiffany Ertle,
Homosassa, Florida

This blend attracts so many birds—cardinals, blue jays, nuthatches, goldfinches and more! I combine safflower seeds, sunflower seeds, thistle, nuts, raisins and lastly, dried cranberries.

—Kathy Lorigan,
Easton, Pennsylvania

I buy cracked corn and black oil sunflower seed in bulk, store it in large plastic containers and then use an auger to mix the two seeds together as we need it. It saves money and we only have to pay for the seed we want to serve the birds.

—Kathy Eppers,
Aledo, Texas

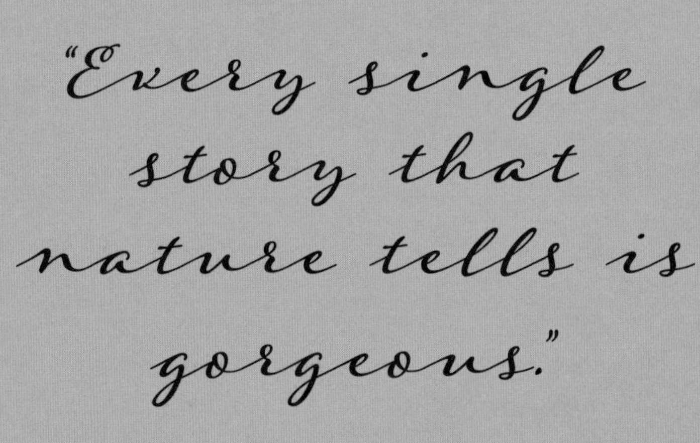

"Every single
story that
nature tells is
gorgeous."

—NATALIE ANGIER

ROLF NUSSBAUMER/ROLFNP.COM

Black-capped chickadee

CHAPTER 3

Stop to Appreciate the Beauty

FROM BRIGHT FEATHERS TO PAPER-THIN WINGS, NATURE'S WONDROUS COLORS AND STRUCTURES ARE YOURS TO ENJOY.

Why do your favorite backyard fliers and furry friends—from birds to bumblebees—appear the way they do? How do their physical characteristics benefit them? Read on for the answers. Plus, you'll learn how to tell apart commonly confused birds, meet the major "families" of butterflies and discover the differences between bees and wasps.

Leucistic female northern cardinal

WHAT'S UP WITH THOSE COLORS?

The hue of a bird's unique feathers and plumage depends on their pigments.

Melanins

Most of the black, gray, brown and reddish brown tones in feathers are created by pigments called melanins. If these pigments are missing, feathers may grow in pure white.

While a lack of melanin leads to white feathers, it is also possible for birds to have an excess of dark pigment. Extra dark, or melanistic, individuals are fairly common in some hawk species, and it's part of their normal variation.

◄ LEUCISTIC

In cases of missing melanins, birds might have just a few white feathers, large random spots of them—or they might look completely white. All of these individuals are known as leucistic.

Splotchy white birds are also sometimes called partial albinos, but scientists disagree on whether this is a valid term. A true albino bird lacks all pigments; it would have white feathers and pink eyes (from blood vessels showing through). Genuine albinos rarely live long in the wild, so birders don't see them often.

BILL & SHARON DRAKER

Carotenoids

Other variations in color are caused by carotenoids, which create red, orange and yellow feathers. Carotenoid colors often show odd variations, too, as in the rare male northern cardinals that are bright yellow instead of red.

Another example of carotenoids causing variations: Male house finches are usually bright red on the chest, but if they have a poor diet, their new feathers grow in orange and yellow. And if cedar waxwings eat the fruits from certain exotic plants, the tips of their tail feathers are known to turn red instead of the usual yellow.

Indigo bunting molting

Balding northern cardinal

Fewer feathers

◀ MOLTING VARIATIONS

A bird might also be partially bald because it is molting. As a very general rule, a healthy wild bird's new feathers will be the same colors as the ones they're replacing, so the effect isn't obvious. But some species change colors with the seasons, or as they become adults.

▲ GOING BALD?

Sometimes, feathers are absent completely! If you've ever spotted a northern cardinal or blue jay with a mostly bald head, the bird isn't sick—don't worry. It might be afflicted with tiny parasites that cause some feathers to fall out. Most birds survive and grow back a full head of feathers in a few weeks.

Golden eagle

BEAK BREAK! TOP 7 BEAK FACTS

They're for tapping, snacking and so much more.

1 ◄ **HELPFUL HOOKS**
Meat-eating birds such as hawks and eagles have hooked beaks that allow them to tear up their meals. But they aren't the only ones with this special feature—vireos use their hooked beaks to help them hunt for caterpillars.

2 **Woodpecker beaks are** built for action. Designed to withstand repeated hammering, they can handle intense pressure. Between its beak and its skull shape, which perfectly protects its brain, a woodpecker doesn't have to worry about getting a concussion while boring for food or making a home.

STEVE AND DAVE MASLOWSKI

4 ▼ CONE POWER

Cone shapes have special abilities. Birds that have cone-shaped beaks have the ability to trap a seed, thanks to a special groove in their beaks, and crack it open. Using their tongues, these birds then nimbly separate the seed from the shell.

3 ► GETTING CROSS

Crossbills can pry open cones. When you look at a crossbill's face, it's obvious how it got its name. The bill is thick at the base, but the mandibles cross over each other instead of meeting at their narrow tips. This shape would be awkward for picking up most items, but it's perfect for one thing—prying open the cones of pines, spruces, hemlocks and other evergreens.

Red crossbill

BOBKOTHENBEUTEL

5 **Skinny beaks get** the worms. A slender beak comes in handy for the white ibis, as it uses it to probe for insects, worms and crustaceans in mud and shallow water.

6 ▲ **UNDERBITES ARE ALL RIGHT**

Some birds, like the black skimmer, seem to have an underbite. But that's not a hindrance—in fact, it helps them catch their food in a very distinct way. They fly while dragging their lower mandibles through water, hoping to scoop up a fish.

7 ▼ SOME BEAKS HAVE SENSES

The long, straight bills of snipes and woodcocks provide a clue to their feeding behavior. They locate food with their sense of touch: The tip of the bill is very sensitive, so when a bird plunges it into the mud, it can feel earthworms, grubs, snails and small creatures moving around. And the upper mandible of the bill is flexible, so these odd birds can open up their bills just at the tip to grab something that's buried deep underground.

Wilson's snipe

FOTOREQUEST/SHUTTERSTOCK

Yellow-headed blackbird

LET'S WING IT

Bird wings are incredibly complex—and vital to their survival. Here is some bite-sized wing wisdom for you to discover.

◀ MUSCLE CONTROL
The average bird wing is a complicated thing. The bone-and-muscle part is relatively small, and most of the visible surface area is composed only of strong feathers. Thanks to the muscles, birds have the ability to constantly change the shape and angle of their wings for masterful control in the air.

BOB KOTHENBEUTEL

▶ AMERICAN GOLDFINCH

Typical songbirds make many short flights every day and may fly long distances during migration. Their wings are slightly pointed, and just large enough to fit their incredibly active lifestyles.

The wings of birds that don't take to the air aren't useless, though. An ostrich dashing across the African plains sticks its stubby, fluffy wings out to the side to help balance during high-speed turns. Penguins use theirs as flippers to propel them in powerful, graceful swimming—in effect "flying" underwater.

American goldfinch

BOB KOTHENBEUTEL

Birds that spend a lot of time soaring over land have long and wide wings. Vultures, eagles and red-tailed hawks are good examples of habitual soarers. As the sun warms the land, it creates currents of rising warm air called thermals. Soaring birds hitch a ride on these thermals, circling up into the sky without any effort.

▲ ABOVE THE SEA

Large seabirds often have very narrow wings. Albatrosses, such as the black-footed albatross commonly seen off our Pacific Coast, maneuver easily in strong winds with their incredibly long, thin wings. Another narrow-winged seabird, the magnificent frigatebird, soars over the Florida Keys and elsewhere on the Florida coast. Recent research shows frigatebirds can fly for days or even weeks at a time without landing—even sleeping mid-flight, while they soar high above tropical ocean waters.

There is tremendous diversity in the shapes of wings, and the differences relate to how the birds use them. A ground-dwelling bird like a northern bobwhite gets around mostly by walking, and only occasionally has to make a quick flight to scurry away from danger. Its wings are very short and rounded, ideal for a rapid escape but not for sustained flight. On the other hand, a barn swallow spends most of the day in the air, swooping about gracefully to catch flying insects. Its wings are longer than its body and sharply pointed.

Waddling, Hopping, Perching

Birds' feet vary by species. Here's how your favorite feathered friends use them.

Ducks and other waterfowl have webbed feet to propel them through the water.

Birds of prey are armed with sharp hooked talons for catching and killing.

Wading birds such as herons have wide feet to support them on sticky mud without sinking.

Songbirds have delicate grasping feet for clutching the tree branches where they perch.

Woodpeckers and their relatives have zygodactyl feet—with two toes pointing forward and two backward—which allow them to cling to and move up and down tree trunks.

Mockingbird family in a rose bush

HOW BIRDS SEE THE WORLD

Surprisingly, they're able to glimpse certain things that humans can't.

◀ **SEEING THE LIGHT**
Birds are able to see ultraviolet light. To us, male and female northern mockingbirds look exactly the same—but birds are able to tell the difference because the two have different ultraviolet markings. In addition, birds can sense the Earth's magnetic field. This ability to judge north and south is clearly helpful as they navigate the sky, especially in migration seasons.

Birds use their excellent color vision to find food, such as ripe fruits and flowers. Their colorful plumage is important in courtship. Studies have shown that when given a choice, female birds often prefer males with the most colorful feathers. There's a catch, though: Night birds such as owls may have a biological trade-off. They see very well in dim light, but their perception of colors may not be as good.

KRISTIN KELLY

All the Better to Hear You With

Yes, birds do have ears—but they might not look exactly how you imagined.

In fact, you might not even see bird ears, because they usually aren't visible. They're on the sides of their heads. The openings are located below and behind the eyes, hidden by feathers.

What aren't ears are the "horns" on top of the great horned owl's head. They are feather tufts called plumicorns. Scientists theorize that owls use them to recognize each other.

Birds see frame by frame. Here's a metaphor to help explain how quickly birds take in the world: When you watch a film, the projector may show 24 frames every second, but your eyes blend them together so you see smooth, continuous motion on the screen. For a bird, the same film would look like a quick series of separate pictures.

The term "eagle-eyed" for sharp vision is no accident. Nearly all birds see at least two or three times as much detail as humans, making them able to spot food—or approaching predators—that much farther away.

Windows are not a bird's best friend. Glass is not only clear; it's reflective. Sky and trees are mirrored in windows, and since there was no such thing as glass in the natural world for the millions of years that birds have been evolving, few wild birds have yet evolved any ability to notice it.

▶ ATYPICAL EYES

Owls' prominent yellow or dark eyes may seem round and nearly humanlike, but owls' eyeballs are actually tube-shaped and cannot move in the sockets. They also have three different eyelids to keep those peepers healthy and clean. To make up for their static eyes, owls are able to rotate their heads an astounding 270 degrees.

BEE CHEAT SHEET

Run from them or love them, there's so much buzz about these endlessly fascinating insects.

Cold doesn't bug them. In cold temperatures, bumblebees can shiver to bring their bodies to their minimum flight temperature of 86 degrees.

▶ NO STEREOTYPES, PLEASE

Native bees can look different from how we often visualize these flying insects. They exist in an array of colors, including metallic green, brown, black, and gray, as well as the stereotypical yellow and black stripes.

DAVE WELLING

Honeybee

Sweat bee

ROBBY W/SHUTTERSTOCK

Bees are not all meanies. Contrary to popular belief, native bees tend to be docile. "Many can't sting humans," says Heather Holm, author of *Pollinators of Native Plants*. "Their stingers can't pierce our skin."

◀ SO SMALL
Some are tiny! Native bees can be quite small and are often mistaken for flies.

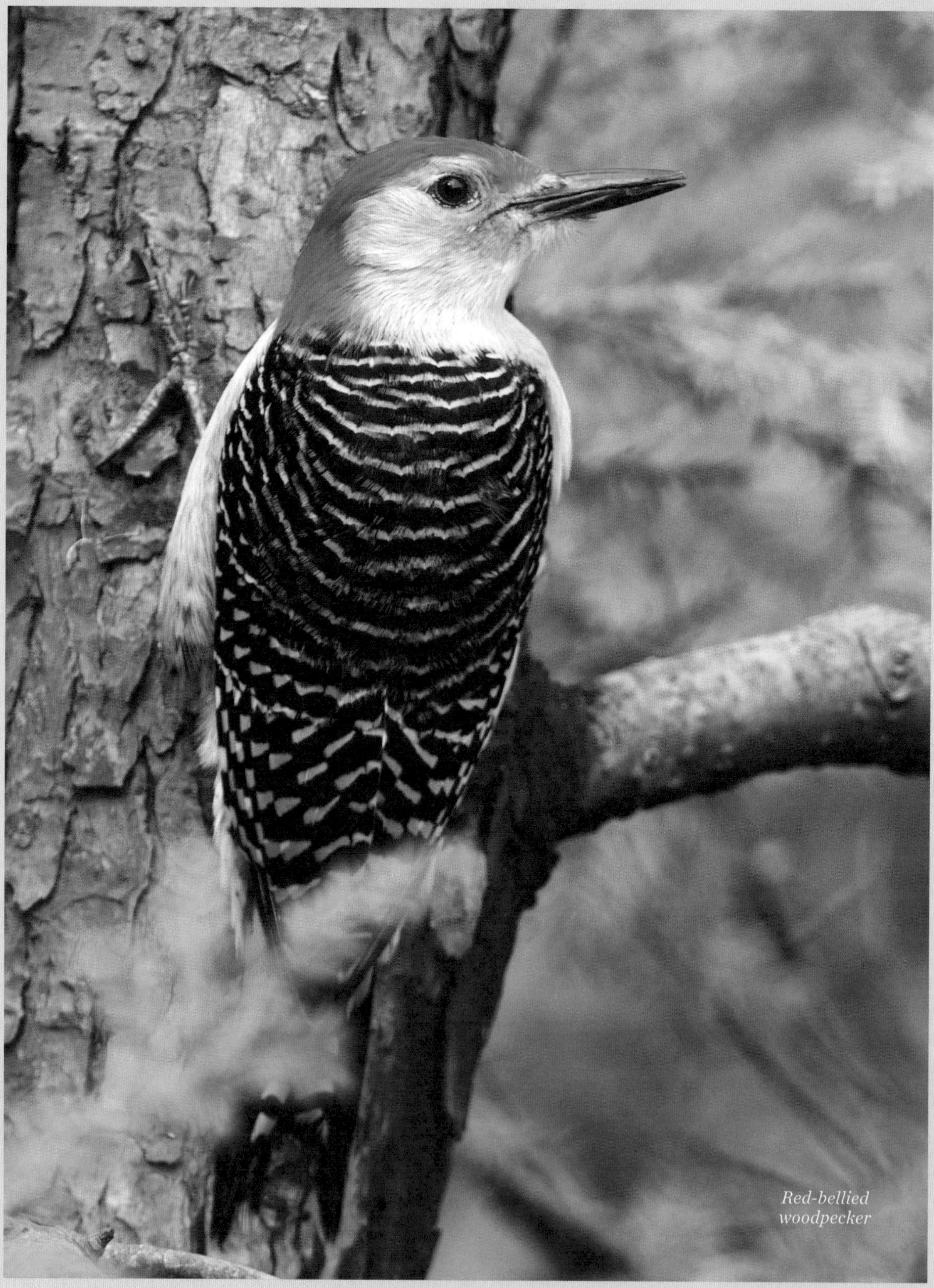

Red-bellied woodpecker

"In order to see birds it is necessary to become part of the silence."

—ROBERT LYND

STEVE AND DAVE MASLOWSKI

Flying squirrel

OTHER BACKYARD CREATURES

Sometimes cute, sometimes squirrelly, sometimes downright surprising, the critters that come to visit are worth getting to know.

◀ FLYING SQUIRRELS

They're active all winter, but you've probably never seen one because they're nocturnal. Unlike their cousins the gray squirrels, flying squirrels rarely come down to the ground. These cute little tree rodents are omnivores, but when insects and birds' eggs aren't available in winter, they subsist on the normal squirrel fare of seeds and nuts.

Weasel in winter

MICHAL PESATA/SHUTTERSTOCK

◀ WEASELS, MINK AND FISHERS

These belong to the mustelid family. These cousins range from the least weasel, weighing less than 2 ounces, to the fisher, which can weigh more than 10 pounds. The most common is the long-tailed weasel, found across the country.

▼ GRAY SQUIRRELS

These bushy-tailed creatures can fall 100 feet without serious injury and are faster than you might think—at top speed, they can run 20 mph. Many gray squirrels are able to jump 8 feet high from a stationary sitting position!

COMMONLY CONFUSED

Avoid a backyard mix-up. Learn how to tell similar-looking birds apart.

▶ HAIRY AND DOWNY WOODPECKERS

Males both have a red spot on the back of the head; a reliable identifier is the shape of the bill. The hairy has a long spear, almost as long as its head, compared to a short, sharp point on the downy. With a close view, the downy usually shows black spots on the white outer tail feathers, while the hairy typically doesn't have these spots.

MARIE READ

Downy woodpecker (at left) and hairy woodpecker (at right).

Ruby-crowned kinglet

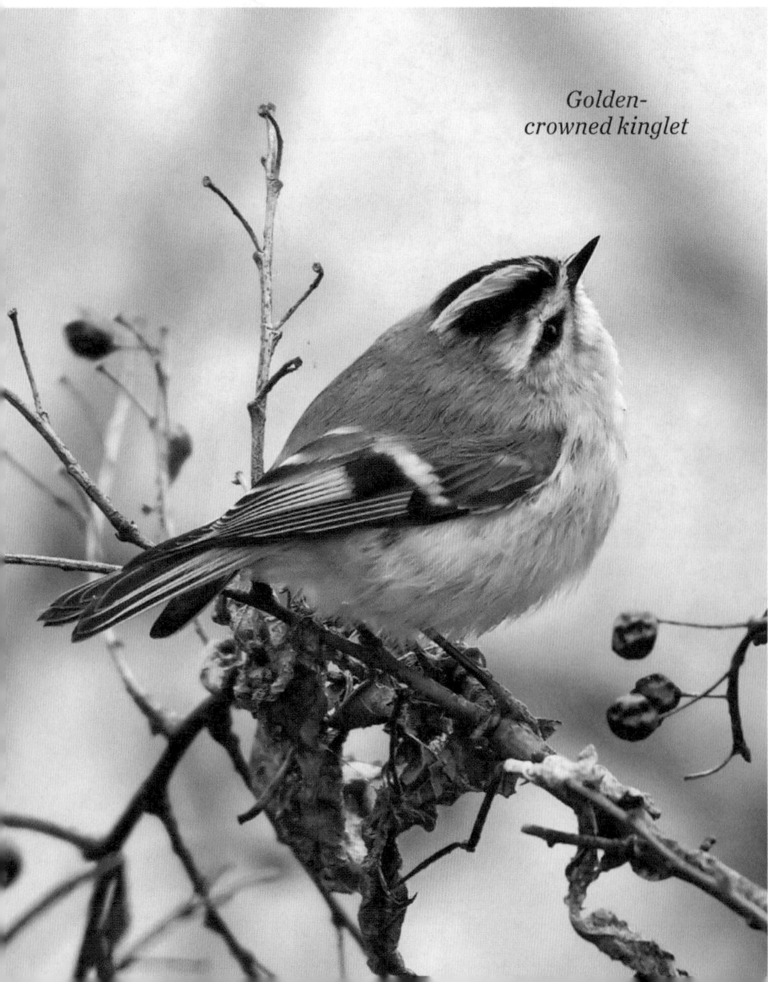

Golden-crowned kinglet

◀ GOLDEN- AND RUBY-CROWNED KINGLETS

Both show one obvious white wing bar bordered with black. Red plumage of the ruby-crown is seen only on the male and is often hidden by other feathers. The golden-crown shows a patch that is yellow or yellow and orange. For an easier field mark, look at their faces. The ruby-crown has a white eye ring. The golden-crown has a white eyebrow topped by a black stripe along the side of its crown.

TOP: BOB KOTHENBEUTEL; BOTTOM: RICHARD BUQUOI

▶ CHIPPING AND AMERICAN TREE SPARROWS

The tree sparrow is slightly larger, with more obvious white wing bars. The stripe behind its eye is reddish brown, not black or dark gray as on the chipping sparrow. Note different bill colors as well: They are bicolored black and yellow on tree sparrows, while chipping sparrows' bills are black in summer and partly dull pink in winter.

Chipping sparrow

American tree sparrow

TOP: ROBERTHARDING/ALAMY STOCK PHOTO; BOTTOM: FRANCIS & JANICE BERGQUIST

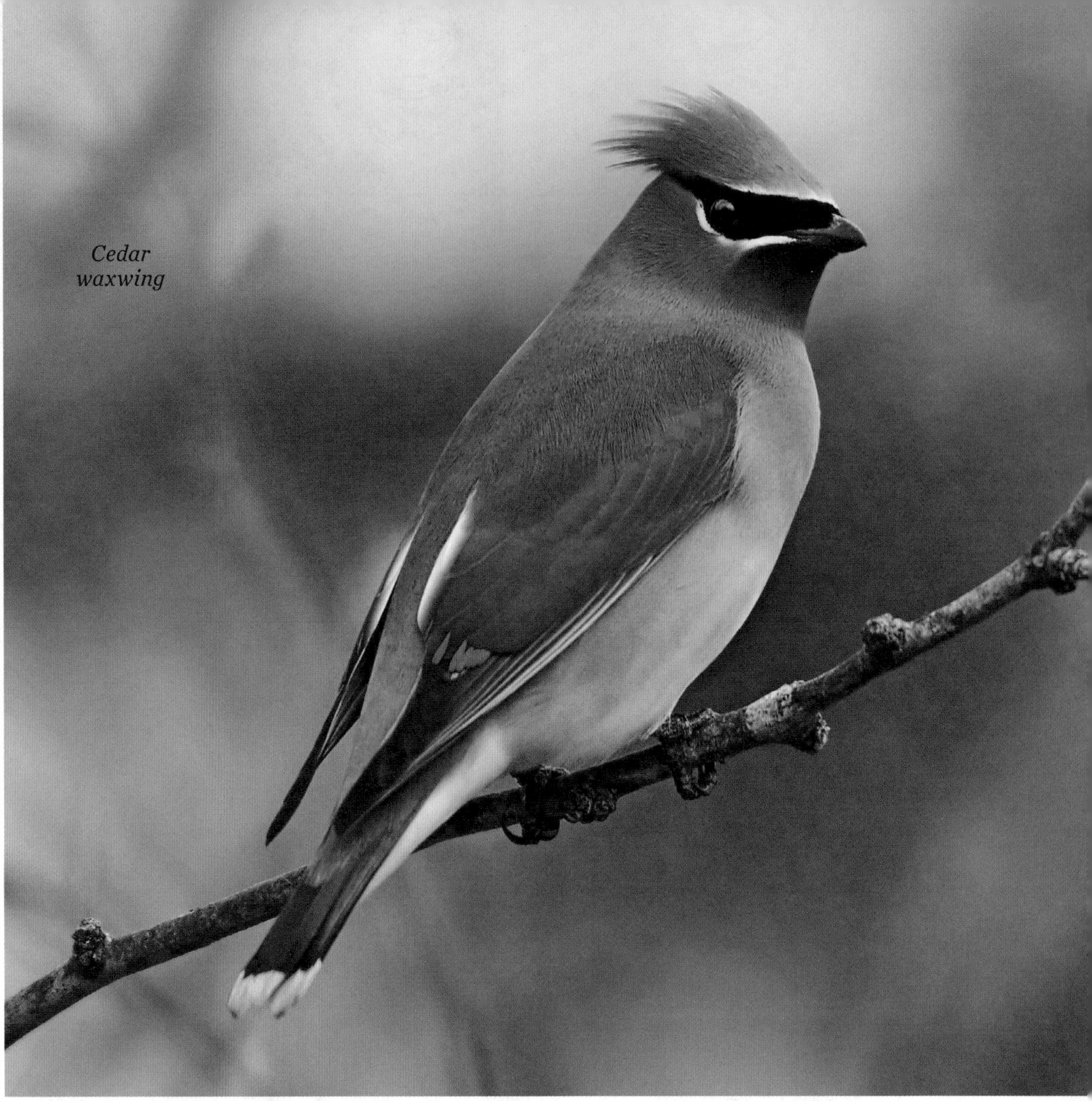

Cedar waxwing

▲ CEDAR AND BOHEMIAN WAXWINGS

They both have bright yellow tail tips, wander in flocks and feast on berries. Both birds are named for the red tips on their wings, but Bohemians also have yellow and white wing markings. Look for a reddish tinge on the face of Bohemians, but the key area to check is under the tail—Bohemians have bright reddish-brown coloring there, while on cedar waxwings, those feathers are plain white.

RICHARD BUQUOI

Bohemian waxwing

DONALD M. JONES/MINDEN PICTURES

Barn swallow

Cliff swallow

◀ **CLIFF AND BARN SWALLOWS**

Tail shape is what separates these birds in flight—the barn swallow has a long forked tail with white spots, while the cliff swallow's tail is short. The forehead can be white or brown on cliff swallows, but a barn swallow's is always reddish brown. Look for the cliff swallow's pale buff-colored lower back and rump, and pale collar across the back of the neck; the barn swallow's back is solidly dark blue, head to tail.

BOTH: BOB KOTHENBEUTEL

Secrets to Bird ID

Make note of these key clues.

SHAPE
Observe the bird's bill and body shape, as well as tail and leg length.

SIZE
Compare the bird's size to another known species, if possible.

LOCATION
Range, season and habitat all help narrow down the likely choices.

BEHAVIOR
Be sure to notice whether the bird is hopping on the ground, soaring, climbing trees or doing something else that's notable.

FIELD MARKS
Pay close attention to stripes on the body, wing bars, eye rings, and head stripes or spots.

COLOR
Any bright or unusual colors might help clinch the ID.

FAMILY INTRODUCTIONS

Every butterfly has a family tree. Which family does your backyard visitor belong to? Take a closer look here.

Painted lady butterflies

Orange sulphur

◀ BRUSHFOOTS

Wingspan: ⅞ to 4 inches

The brushfoot (*Nymphalidae*) family gets its name from the short hairs covering the tiny front legs of its members. A diverse range of fliers are part of this group, including fritillaries, painted ladies, crescents, admirals and monarchs.

▲ WHITES AND SULPHURS

Wingspan: 1 to 3 inches

If you've seen a dainty white or yellow butterfly visiting your flower garden, it's probably a member of the *Pieridae* family, which includes whites, sulphurs and orangetips. Some southern members of this group wander far north in summer and fall.

LEFT: RICK SCHMIDT; RIGHT: DENNIS COLBERT

Eastern tiger swallowtail

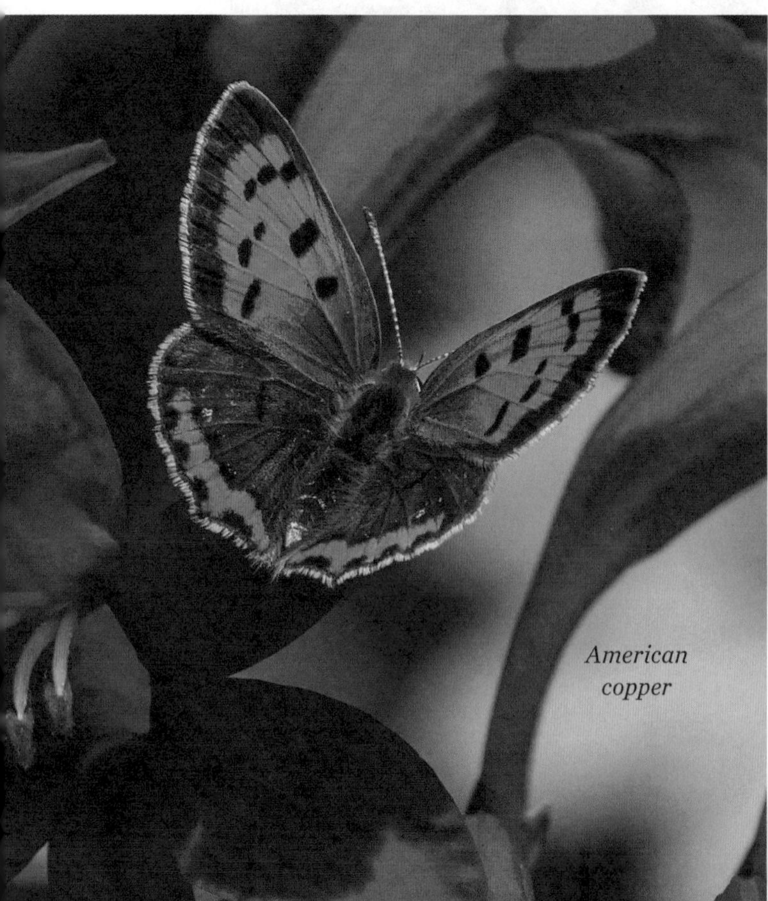

American copper

◀ GOSSAMER-WINGED

Wingspan: ⅔ to 2 inches

Four distinct North American groups are part of the *Lycaenidae* family: coppers, hairstreaks, harvesters and blues. Many in the gossamer-winged group have eyespots and short extensions on their hindwings to fool predators into grabbing the wrong end, which makes escape easier.

TOP: NINA EHMER; BOTTOM: GLENN TRAVER

◀ **SWALLOWTAILS**

Wingspan: 2 to 5 inches

The biggest butterflies in North America are part of the swallowtail (*Papilionidae*) family. Their most familiar members are the eastern and western tigers, which, like most swallowtails, have a long taillike extension on both hindwings. But some species in this family are actually tailless, notably the parnassians.

Where Do All Those Colors Come From?

You'd never guess—it's scales.

If you put a butterfly wing under a microscope, you'll see that it's covered in many tiny scales, which give the butterfly its magnificent colors and patterns. Underneath the scales are thin layers of protein called chitin, which is also found in octopus beaks, insect exoskeletons, fish scales and more.

MONARCH LOOK-ALIKES

You can detect the subtle differences among a trio of backyard fliers that look like monarchs.

▶ SIGNS OF THE REAL DEAL

Look for light orange wings with thick black veins and small white dots along edges of the wings to tell if you're seeing a monarch. Male monarchs have two black dots on their hindwings. You can spot monarchs all across the U.S. (though they are less common in the Northwest) and southern Canada.

TERRY STANFILL

Monarch

Meet the Imposters

▼ QUEEN BUTTERFLIES

They have darker, orange-brown wings than monarchs and viceroys. Their wings also feature white dots and inconspicuous dark veins on the upperside. Spot them in the southwestern states, Florida and along the southeastern coast of the United States.

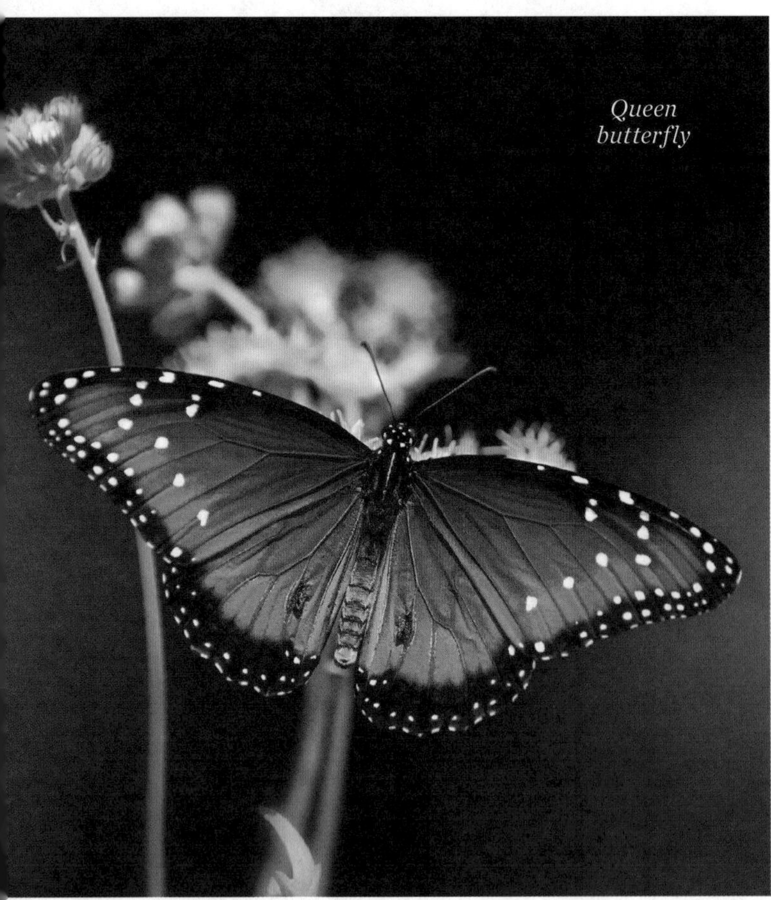

Queen butterfly

▶ VICEROY BUTTERFLIES

They look a lot like monarchs, due to their similar coloring and markings. The main difference to look for is a black stripe across the hindwings. These butterflies are widespread across the U.S. and southern Canada except for parts of the far West.

▶ SOLDIER BUTTERFLIES

They have many markings similar to queens, but they have fewer white dots on top of their forewings. Their wing veins are more prominent than queens. Soldiers are mostly spotted in southern Texas, which is a rare butterfly hot spot, and in Florida. But they are relatively uncommon.

LEENA ROBINSON/ALAMY STOCK PHOTO

Viceroy butterfly

Soldier butterfly

TOP: BOOKGUY/GETTY IMAGES; BOTTOM: JIM AND LYNNE WEBER/SHUTTERSTOCK

DENISE NEUENDORF

Field Notes

Eastern Tiger Swallowtail

I found this butterfly frolicking about in a field of brilliant sunflowers in Meigs County, Tennessee. Its stunning open wings, with so many shades of yellow, perfectly complement the hues of the flower, while the blues balance the color of the vibrant sky.

—Denise Neuendorf, Cleveland, Tennessee

10 KEYS TO BUTTERFLY ID

Take notice of your flying pollinators and learn helpful butterfly identification tips.

1 **Butterflies come in** a variety of colors, sizes and shapes, so make a mental note of these characteristics when you spot a species you don't know.

2 **Even better, take** a photo of your mystery flier so you can look it up later.

3 ▶ **WING WATCH**
Some butterflies have wing shapes or marks that you'll start to recognize by family. Skippers, for instance, have small wings, while longwings have narrow wings, and commas and question marks have "punctuation" on their wings. It's relatively easy to spot the distinctive monarchs, swallowtails and admirals.

Question mark butterfly

4 **A species' region** and habitat are also important butterfly identification tools. Few species are found across the entire continent; some have very limited ranges.

5 **Type of habitat** matters when it comes to identification, too. It's easy to confuse a pipevine swallowtail with a similarly colored red-spotted purple butterfly—unless you know that the former prefers sunny fields and open woodlands and feeds on flower nectar, while the red-spotted purple lives deeper in the forest and feeds on fallen fruits, sap and even dung and carrion.

6 ◀ **MYSTERY SOLVED**
Here's a question to ask when you spot a "mystery" butterfly: Is it really a moth? Many moths are drably colored, but that isn't a foolproof ID because some are just as colorful as butterflies. The sea-foam green of a luna moth and the yellow and pink of an io moth can also be confused with colors found on butterfly wings.

7 **Generally, butterflies are** active during the day, while the majority of moths are nocturnal (with some exceptions). Moth antennae are either feathery or threadlike, while butterfly antennae are smooth and end in a small knob.

8 **You can recognize** a butterfly when not in flight because it folds up its wings over its body while resting. Moths, on the other hand, usually fold their wings down alongside their bodies.

JENNY MINER

9 ▼ **LARVA LOOKOUT** Like the winged adults, caterpillars vary widely in appearance from species to species. Identifying the caterpillars in your garden will tell you which butterflies you can expect to see.

10 **When identifying caterpillars,** pay attention to which plant your caterpillar is eating. Each species can feed upon only a limited number of plants, so knowing the host plant is a big clue.

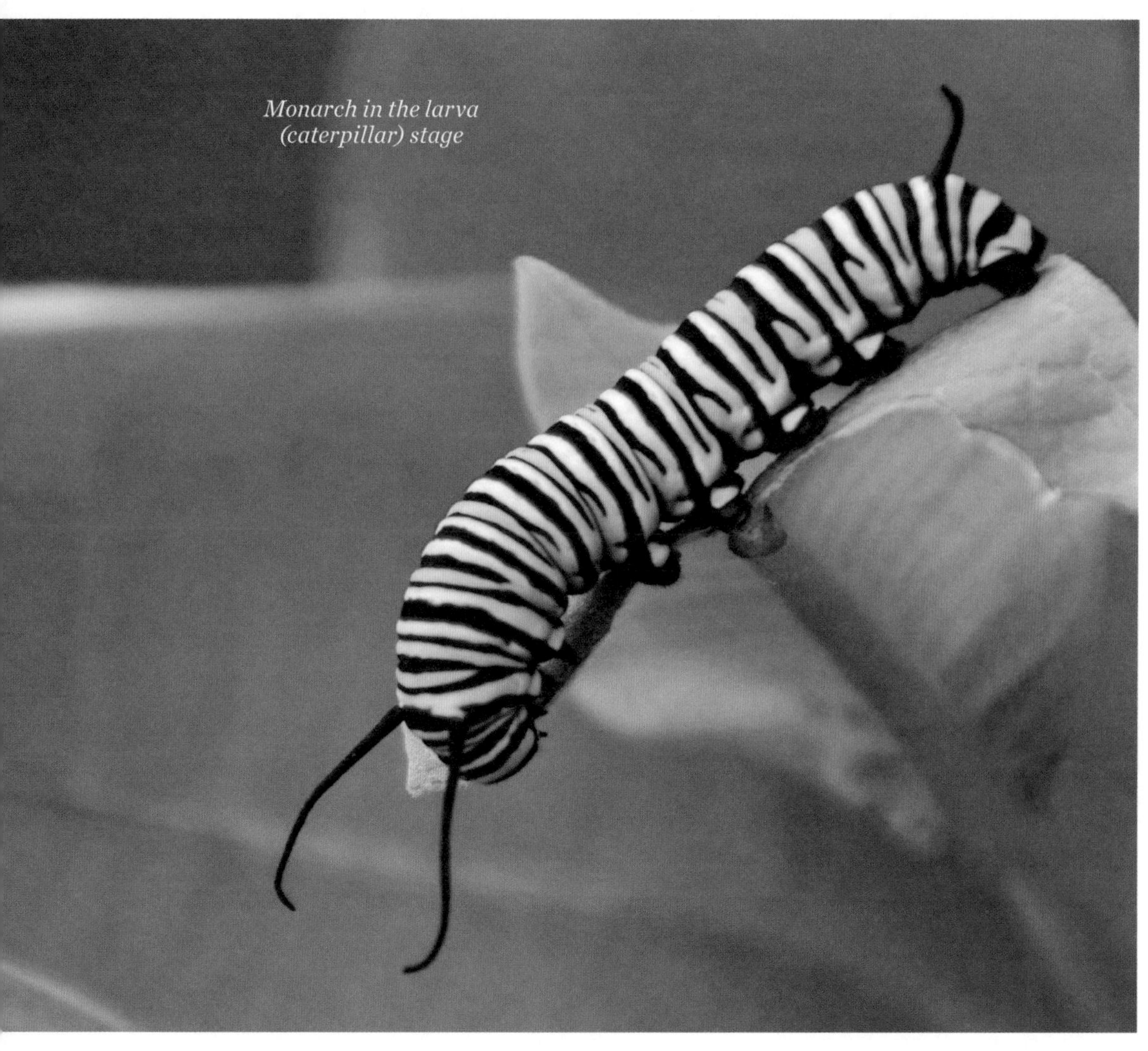

Monarch in the larva (caterpillar) stage

A BEE OR NOT A BEE?

Use this guide to know whether it's a bee or a wasp buzzing through your backyard.

Wasp

▼ STINGER
In the case of wasps, the stinger stays with the insect, meaning it can sting several times.

▼ WINGS
Two sets of wasp wings run parallel to the abdomen when folded down.

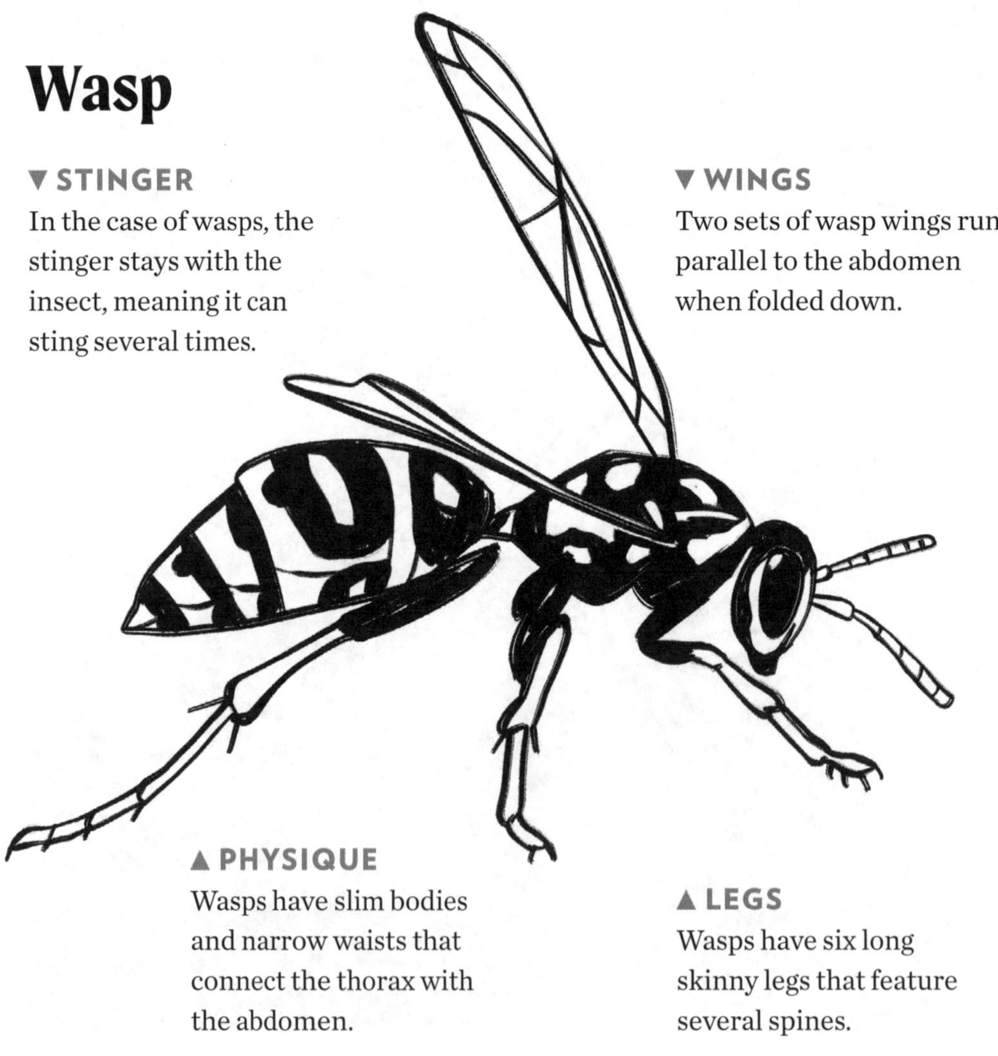

▲ PHYSIQUE
Wasps have slim bodies and narrow waists that connect the thorax with the abdomen.

▲ LEGS
Wasps have six long skinny legs that feature several spines.

As strict nectar and pollen eaters, bees spend most of their time foraging at flowers—and on their best behavior. Wasps are predators that are always on the hunt for their next meal, whether its insects or the food at your barbecue.

Both bees and wasps are pollinators that will visit backyard blooms to sip on sweet nectar.

Bee

▼ PHYSIQUE
Bees have thick, rounded bodies with stripes. Bees have pollen-collecting hair on their bodies, and females also have hair on their legs and bellies.

▼ WINGS
Bees' two sets of wings rest on top of the thorax (middle part of the body) when folded down.

▶ LEGS
Bees have six short bulky legs that are flat, not rounded.

▲ STINGER
A honeybee stinger stays in the victim, meaning the bee eventually dies.

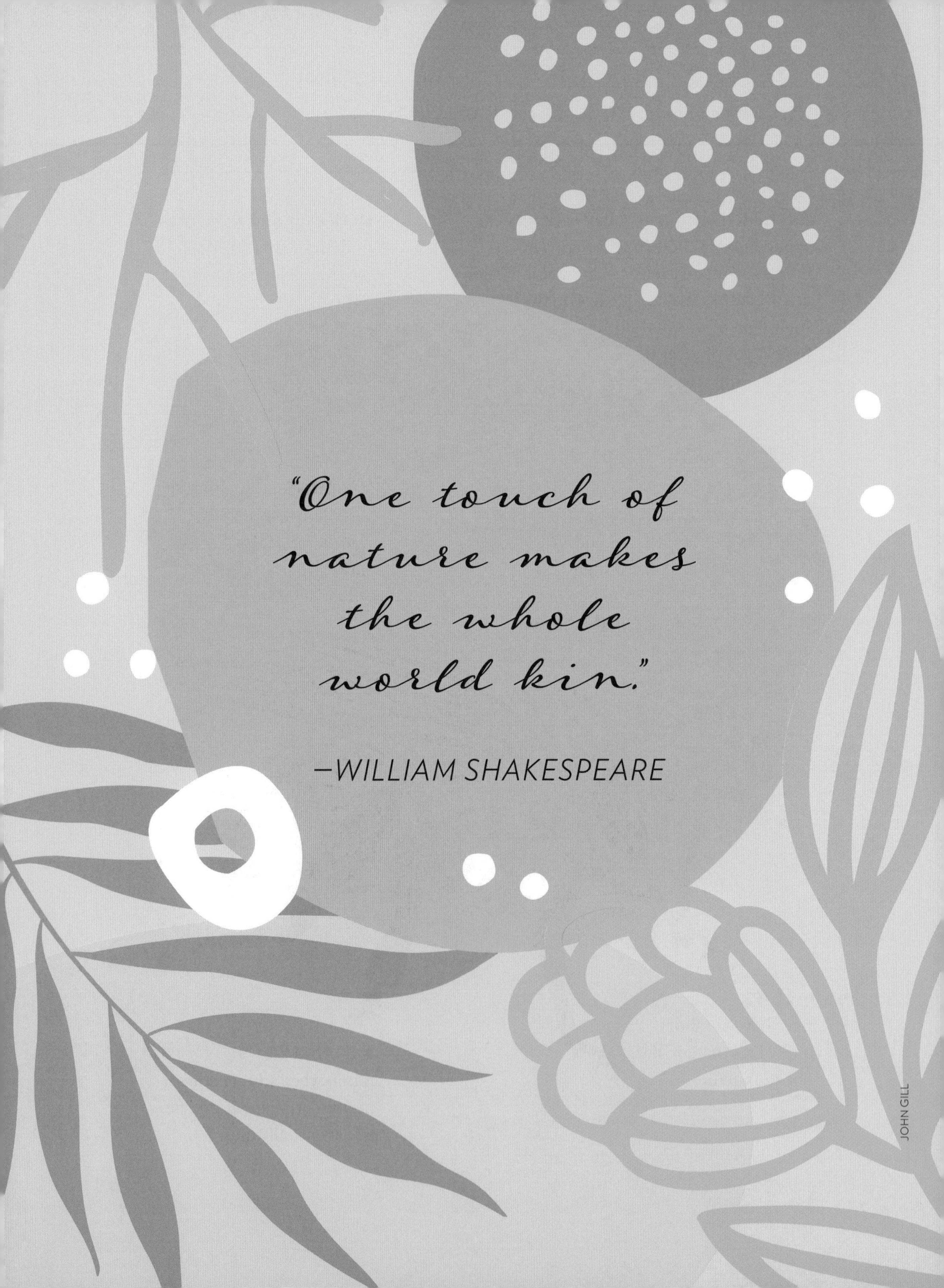
"One touch of nature makes the whole world kin."
—WILLIAM SHAKESPEARE
JOHN GILL

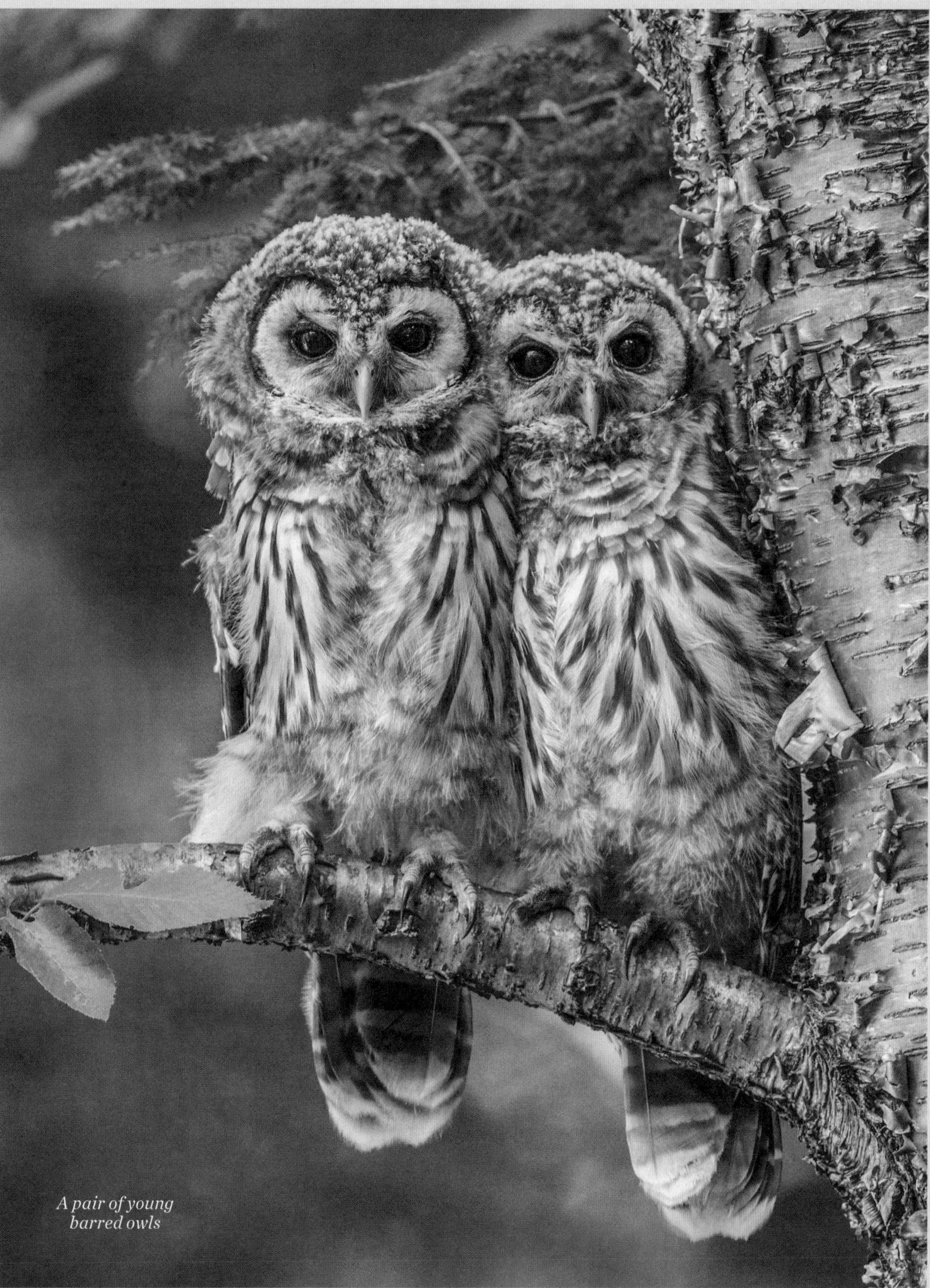

A pair of young barred owls

Ultimate Garden Know-How

CHAPTER 4

THERE'S SOMETHING SPECIAL ABOUT TIME SPENT TENDING TO PLANTS—AND YOU'RE ABOUT TO ENJOY IT SO MUCH MORE.

Let's go behind the leaves. In this chapter, you'll discover how gardens grow and what you can do to help. You'll become a whiz at telling weeds and flowers apart, and learn a variety of ways to keep your plants thriving when the weather shifts. Plus, you'll learn to decipher the spots where the sun shines the brightest, as well as the pesky places where weeds grow.

Banana slug

DIAGNOSING COMMON PLANT PROBLEMS

The doctor is in. Birds & Blooms *plant expert Melinda Myers answers the most common gardening questions.*

◀ ICK, SLUGS. HOW CAN I GET RID OF THEM?

Sink a shallow can filled with beer near your plants, or set a half-empty beer bottle on its side in the garden. Attracted to the fermenting yeast, the slugs crawl into the container and die.

What are these holes in my hostas? Holes in your hosta plants likely came from slugs. But while they're the main culprits, earwigs, hail, frost and even falling maple seeds can pierce those leaves.

ROGER HARRELL

And what about trapping earwigs? Place a piece of crumpled paper under an overturned flowerpot and leave it overnight. In the morning, lift the pot and shake the paper over a can of soapy water.

▼ HOW MUCH WATER DO MY INDOOR PLANTS NEED?

It's all based on type of plant, light exposure, potting mix, temperature and humidity. When in doubt, test the moisture level by sticking your finger into the top 1-2 inches of potting mix. Cacti and succulents like to go a bit drier, while tropical plants prefer consistently moist—not wet—soil.

How can I diagnose my own plant problems?
First, identify the plant and get to know its growing conditions and common ailments. Make sure you've got the preferred soil and are providing the right amounts of water and sun. Next, do an internet search (preferably on a local university or botanical site) for insect and disease problems that are common to the plant.

Goodbye, Powdery Mildew

Here's what this disease is—and how to eliminate it from your garden.

Powdery mildew is a fungal disease that leaves white powder on your plants' leaves. Over time, it blocks sunlight, causing foliage to turn yellow and, in severe cases, drop off.

Fortunately, this disease doesn't usually kill healthy plants, though it does affect appearance and reduce vegetable productivity.

To stop it, plant something a bit shorter in front of the susceptible specimen. The shorter plant masks the mildewed leaves but allows you to enjoy the blossoms.

If you want to take a more aggressive approach, organic products are available. Do a thorough cleanup and discard infected leaves in fall to reduce the source of disease next year.

Stop powdery mildew before it starts by choosing mildew-resistant varieties whenever possible.

Clover

DON'T PULL IT UP!

These plants—which many consider to be weeds—actually add value to your backyard.

◀ CLOVER

Many lawn enthusiasts consider it a weed, but clover is an important source of nectar for bees and a tasty treat for wildlife. Some people grow clover lawns as a more eco-friendly alternative to traditional grass.

MARK TURNER/TURNER PHOTOGRAPHICS

Common purslane. You can use this plant as part of your dinner. This summer annual, which thrives in hot, dry conditions, is a tasty substitute for spinach. Pull it before it sets seed to keep it under control, but throw a little on your salad, too.

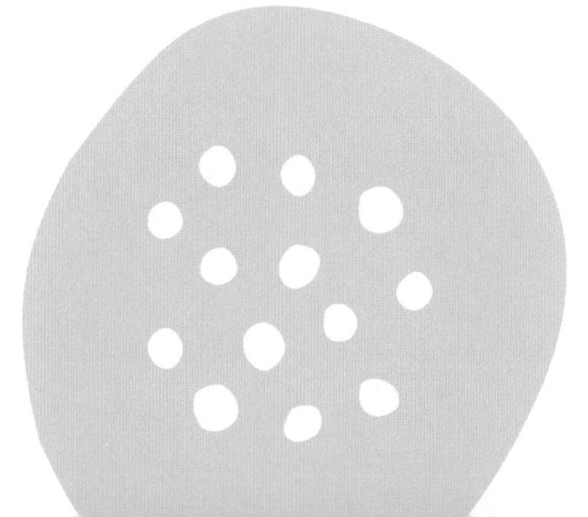

▼ LAMB'S QUARTERS

This plant can be tasty—but research before you chow down. Lamb's quarters is moving off many weed lists and onto gourmet restaurant menus. But do a little reading before you eat: Too much can make you sick.

CHICKWEED

Spice up your salad with chickweed. This is another one that can quickly take over a garden, but it adds zing to a salad or sandwich.

Dandelions. Many homeowners tirelessly remove dandelions from their lawns, but nature loves it, and it's not as bad as people think. Birds eat the seeds, and the leaves have long been used in early-spring salads because they're rich in vitamin C.

AVOFERTEN/SHUTTERSTOCK

Dame's rocket

WEED ID

Here's how to identify and eliminate the most common leafy pests.

◀ DAME'S ROCKET

Look for four-petaled flowers on dame's rocket. Dame's rocket is tricky; it looks pretty blooming in spring, but this nonnative weed is often included in wildflower mixes, and it quickly crowds out more desirable native plants. Look for the four-petaled flowers that distinguish this from the five-petaled flowers of phlox—and then get rid of it.

Teasle. A thistle look-alike, teasle has prickly stems and leaves that make it undesirable to both wildlife and agriculture. If you find it in your backyard, you'll want to eliminate it.

MARK TURNER/TURNER PHOTOGRAPHICS

▲ **POISON IVY**
"Leaves of three, let it be" is the best advice for poison ivy—the ultimate weed to avoid. All parts of poison ivy can cause an allergic reaction. You may stumble on it during a hike or find it along the ground or crawling up a tree. Wear protective clothing and wash thoroughly after touching it.

Field bindweed. Get this bothersome plant under control early. Field bindweed has flowers like a morning glory, and a deep root system, which makes it drought tolerant and difficult to eliminate. Your best bet is to keep pulling the weeds as early as possible. Mulching will also help prevent the seeds from sprouting.

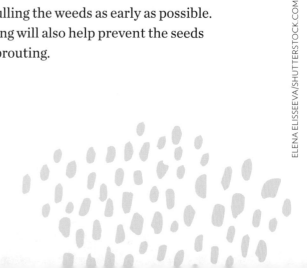

ELENA ELISSEEVA/SHUTTERSTOCK.COM

Quack grass. If you try to remove quack grass by hand, you'll have to be determined. It is easy to identify by the long, white underground rhizomes that look like roots. Any piece of the rhizome that touches the ground can start a new plant.

▼ RAGWEED

Allergy sufferers will want to eliminate ragweed. You can usually find this pesky weed hiding behind its colorful neighbor, goldenrod. Be sure to mow it down or pull it before it has a chance to release its allergenic pollen.

Ragweed

PURPLE LOOSESTRIFE

Buckthorn, garlic mustard and purple loosestrife are detrimental to wildlife. These weeds were once prized landscape plants, but they now crowd out native plants and disrupt natural ecosystems. It's definitely worth your time and energy to try to get rid of them. Their presence reduces food sources and habitat for native birds, butterflies, beneficial insects and wildlife.

ANNA GRATYS/SHUTTERSTOCK

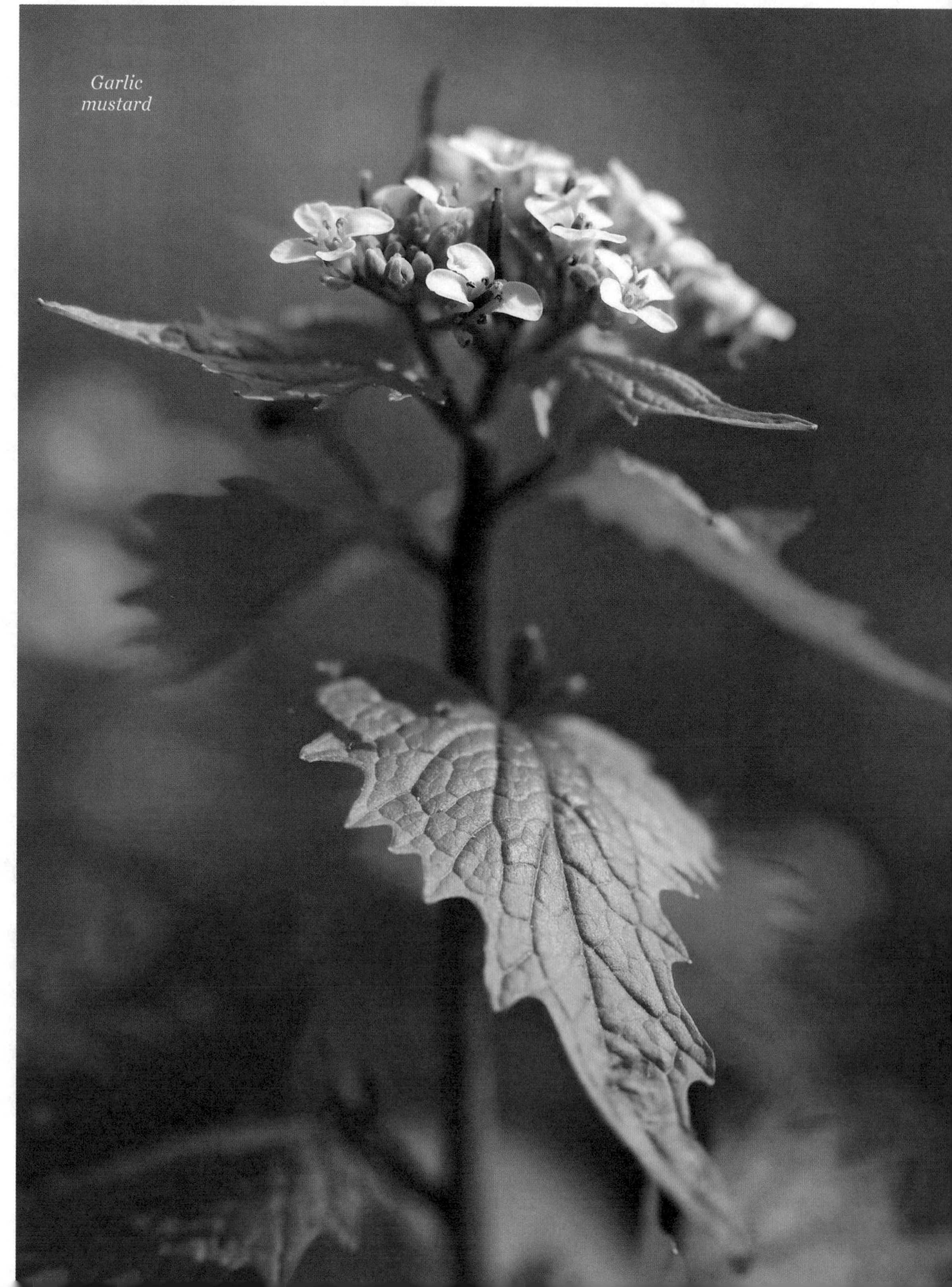

Garlic mustard

◀ **GARLIC MUSTARD**
This notorious forest invader was brought here for medicinal purposes and food. A relative of mustard, this biennial plant produces thousands of seeds that can stay in the soil for seven years or more. Pull and properly dispose of plants just before they flower.

Creeping Charlie. This weed is easy to identify by its round scalloped leaves, which are fragrant when crushed. This shade-tolerant plant with purple spring flowers can quickly take over a lawn or garden bed. To get rid of it in the lawn, try a chelated iron-based weedkiller. In the garden, pull it out and mulch, or use a total vegetation killer.

ISTOCKPHOTO.COM/TACOJIM

Flower vs. Weed

If a mystery plant fits any or all of these descriptions, you may have a weed on your hands:

- It's multiplied considerably since last year.
- It's sprouted up throughout the bed and lawn.
- It has been in the garden for a few years, never seems to bloom and has unimpressive foliage. (But remember: Perennials and biennials do not bloom in the first summer, and some plants need a few years to establish and flower.)
- You don't like it. Sometimes, it's simply a matter of taste, so find a gardener willing to take an ugly duckling off your hands.

TOP 10 WAYS GARDENING HELPS YOU LIVE BETTER

Whether you're out yanking weeds or watering tomatoes, there are plenty of surprising ways that gardening is good for you, your family and your wallet.

MARTIN POOLE/GETTY IMAGES

1 ◀ YOU GET A POWER BOOST

It's a great way to up your "power foods." Foods low in calories but high in nutrients that fight heart disease can be grown in your backyard. Some to try are asparagus, broccoli, avocado, bell peppers, carrots, leafy greens, tomatoes and squash.

2 Forty-five minutes of gardening burns as many calories as a 30-minute aerobic activity. Weeding, digging and planting can burn as many as 350 calories per hour. It's fun exercise that gets you outdoors, listening to the birds instead of being cooped up in the gym.

RAWPIXEL.COM/SHUTTERSTOCK

3 ◄ **SAVE MONEY** You can noticeably trim your grocery bill by growing just a few of your favorite vegetables. Plus, store-bought veggies just don't taste as good as homegrown!

4 **It improves your** strength and motor skills. Low-impact exercises such as digging, weeding and planting strengthen muscles and are a good choice for those who can't participate in vigorous activity. Also, gardening uses many muscle groups as well as promoting hand strength, joint flexibility and improved motor skills.

5 ◀ YOU'RE BEING ACTIVE!

Tending to your plants keeps your heart healthy. Research has proven that light physical activity significantly lowers the risk of heart disease.

6

Gardening helps you get a daily dose of vitamin D. Obtained through exposure to sunlight, this vitamin protects against health problems like osteoporosis, heart disease, stroke and cancer.

7

It's good for you. Spending time outside, even in short spurts, can do wonders for your mood, reducing stress and tension and helping you relax.

8 ▶ YOU'LL SLEEP BETTER

If you want a good night's rest, eat a diet rich in vegetables and add light exercise and fresh air. (If you still have trouble getting your zzz's, plant lavender in your backyard—it promotes relaxation.)

AUREMAR/SHUTTERSTOCK

9 ▶ THERE'S KID APPEAL

Growing veggies may get your kids interested in eating them! Try unusually colored ones. They might just eat that crazy purple carrot because, well, it's a purple carrot!

10 **Gardening is a** nice break from screen time. Instead of rushing home to video games and TV, anyone—namely the kiddos in your bunch—can pick up gardening gear, go on a frog hunt or simply sit and count butterflies.

BOKAN/SHUTTERSTOCK

Monarch

"Who has learned to garden who did not at the same time learn to be patient?"
—H.L.V. FLETCHER
DESIGN PICS INC/ALAMY STOCK PHOTO

EDIBLE PETALS

Yes, it's possible to have flowers for dinner. Take our tips on how to freshen up meals with blooms from your backyard.

Nibble only on those types you know are safe to consume, since not all flowers are edible. And always be sure to double-check that the flowers are grown organically—no pesticides, please.

▶ WOW FACTOR
Add interest to your dishes. Flowers can really brighten up a meal, and the absolute easiest way to use edible flowers is as garnish on plates or on soups.

Harvest flowers immediately before using. Why? They wilt quickly. You can dry flower petals by hanging stems in a warm space with good air circulation, or by placing individual flowers or petals on a fine mesh; store the dried blooms as if they were spices, in airtight glass containers kept in a dark space.

Fresh blooms add color and flavor to salads.

▲ SPICY NASTURTIUMS

Mix flowers in salads, dips, quick breads and butters. Spicy nasturtiums add a peppery bite to greens, while chopped petals look gorgeous blended into a sour cream dip or cream cheese spread. Add flavor to softened butter by stirring in snipped chive blossoms or tiny thyme flowers. Top a white frosted cake with colorful violas or sunflower petals.

Pick your plants with your plates in mind. If you'd like to get dinner from your flower garden, every year, sow seeds of flowering annuals such as nasturtiums, calendulas, pansies and violas, as well as vegetables like zucchini squash. Perennials with edible blooms include roses and daylilies, plus herbs such as chives, sage, lavender and mint.

Be patient. If you purchase a plant that's blooming in a garden center, hold off on taste testing petals until new flowers form so you know for sure that they're chemical-free.

Foraging Basics

It's fun to find natural free food. Just follow these guidelines.

- Ask permission to forage on private property and public lands near you.
- Be certain the food was grown without any chemicals or pollutants.
- Leave some behind for wildlife and to renew the source.
- Test new food in small amounts to learn if it agrees with you.
- Pick carefully. One mistake could endanger your health. If in doubt, contact your county extension office.

SPECIAL SECTION

GARDENING NO MATTER THE WEATHER

Here's how to respond to common weather conditions, as well as sudden shifts and seasonal changes. Plus, discover how to get accurate readings from gardening gadgets.

Drought

Plants develop shallow root systems and become more vulnerable to drought if you water them frequently. Instead, water less often—but slowly and deeply. This encourages deep root growth, which makes plants better able to search out scant moisture in the soil.

Compost goes a long way toward drought-proofing your garden. Use it as a soil amendment and as mulch to help the soil retain moisture, ensuring that your garden plants receive maximum benefit from watering and whatever precipitation you get.

Here are the specifics: Spread a layer of compost about 2 inches (5 cm) deep over beds and dig it 1 to 1½ feet (30 to 45 cm) into the soil before planting; add another layer as mulch afterward.

Compost

ANNIE OTZEN/GETTY IMAGES

Keep color in the yard by planting drought tolerant flowers. Annuals that can withstand dry conditions include gerbera daisies, sunflowers, portulacas, marigolds and zinnias. Perennials to consider include black-eyed Susans, penstemons, coreopsis, evening primroses and yarrow.

Become Thermometer Savvy

There's an art to where you put your thermometers. Follow these guidelines.

For the most accurate reading, put them in spots that receive no direct sunlight. Under certain conditions, a thermometer that is set 5 feet (1.5 meters) above ground can show a temperature up to 15°F (27°C) higher than one at ground level. So if the temperature reads 45°F (7°C) at that height, there can still be frost damage to tender low-growers.

Use a maximum-minimum thermometer, available at most discount and home supply stores, to determine your garden's microclimates. With two separate gauges, it records the highest and lowest temperatures at a certain spot in a given time period.

Sunflower

JEAN OWENS

Heat

Let heat-intolerant veggies such as cauliflower, cabbage, radishes, beets, spinach and peas mature during cool weather by planting them as soon as the soil can be worked in spring. Plant a second crop in late summer. In hot regions they can be planted in late fall for a winter harvest.

Plant tall sun-worshipping plants such as corn, sunflowers or cosmos south of those that need a little shade each day, such as lettuce, spinach and beets. That way, they can serve as shade providers.

Site heat-sensitive ornamentals on the shady side of buildings, next to taller shrubs, or beneath the overhanging branches of trees. Don't plant under shallow-rooted trees, such as maple or beech.

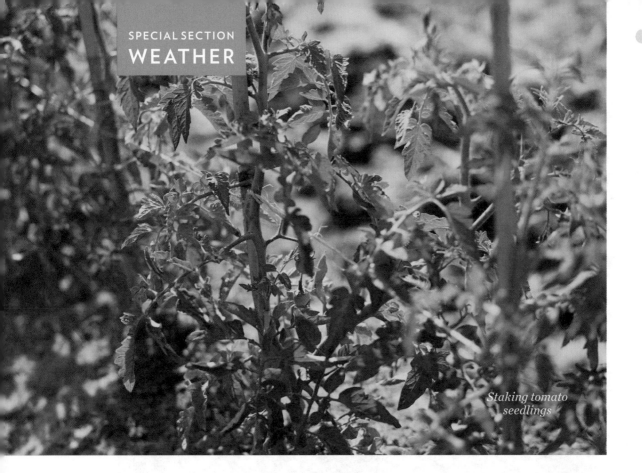

Staking tomato seedlings

Wind

When the wind blows, you can protect young plants by simply hammering a few stakes around them and wrapping a barrier of burlap or a spun-bonded fabric around the stakes.

To protect a small garden from wind damage, make a windbreak with plastic screening. You can buy it by the roll from a lumberyard or garden supply store.

Install stakes or posts on the windward side of the garden and tie or staple the screening to them. A simple windbreak of this sort can reduce the force of the wind by as much as 60%.

Many plants won't tolerate deep planting that would provide extra support on windy days. In that case, there's an alternate solution: Plant them at the recommended depth and then support tall specimens with stakes or cages. As extra insurance, erect a barrier on the windward side.

Snow

Areas of early-melting snow can indicate warm microclimates in your garden. Use them to grow tender plants or as a place to keep seedlings safe from sneaky late frosts.

A hedge trimmed to a flat top may accumulate enough snow to cause branches to split or collapse under the weight. In heavy snowfall areas, protect hedges by cutting them to arched peaks, which naturally shed a heavy blanket of snow.

Gather clean snow in a bucket and take it inside. When it has melted and the water reaches room temperature, use it to water your houseplants. Melted snow is as good as distilled water for plants that are sensitive to fluoride and the salts found in hard water, and as a bonus, it often contains minor nutrients.

Arborvitae bush covered in thick snow piles

Frost

The best defense for hardy plants is mulch. After cold weather arrives, spread 3 inches (8 cm) of shredded bark, leaves or straw to help the soil maintain a steady temperature. Cover with netting, chicken wire or tree branches to protect against wind.

When the first frost is on the way, pull up your tomato plants, shake off the dirt, and hang them upside down from your garage rafters. The fruits will continue to ripen for several weeks.

Protect wall-trained vines, shrubs and trees with a removable shade. Mount a piece of wood at the top of the wall and attach a sheet of canvas to it large enough to cover the plants completely. Let the cloth hang down over the plants in very cold weather. Pull up the shade when it's warm and lower it in late afternoon to conserve heat for the night ahead.

Let a sprinkler play over tender plants all night when a sudden freeze is predicted. Water gives off heat as it turns to ice and will keep the plants warmer than the air. This trick is often used to keep the blossoms on fruit trees from being ruined by late freezes.

Frozen viburnum berries

KARITAP/GETTY IMAGES

5 Ways to Protect Spring Seedlings

Late spring frosts happen. Here's how to protect your vulnerable plants from this unpredictable weather.

1. Cover each with an upside-down flowerpot at night. Small cardboard boxes, held in place with a brick or stone, can be equally effective for rows of plants.
2. Protect cuttings and seedlings in pots with a plastic bag or the top half of a plastic soda bottle, which gets placed over the plants. Remove the cap from the bottle for ventilation.
3. Make a lightweight cover for seedlings with a light wood frame, two crossed hoops of wire, and a covering of clear plastic. If built in several different sizes, the covers can be used for numerous plants and stacked for easy storage.
4. Fill plastic milk jugs with water and place them in planting beds among your seedlings. The sun heats the jugs during the day; at night, these homemade heaters radiate warmth for delicate plants.
5. In the vegetable garden, protect young spring sprouts with floating row covers. Lay the lightweight fabric right over the plants or hold it aloft with sticks or hoops made from heavy-gauge wire. Even lightweight row covers are effective against frost down to 28°F (–2°C).

Grow a Thriving Winter Garden

Answer these vital questions and you'll learn how to green on year-round.

LIVE IN ZONE 8 OR ABOVE?

SURE DO.

Gardeners all over the country envy you! We know you still get some freezing nighttime temps—but those are the exception, not the rule. Don't be afraid to experiment. Just offer a little extra protection on cold nights.

NOT EVEN CLOSE.

We hear ya. You're not going to be planting much of anything outdoors during winter months. Accept it and move on.

DO YOU LIKE HERBS?

WHO DOESN'T?

You can always find a sunny windowsill on which to grow a pot of rosemary, cilantro or basil. If you don't have a good windowsill, try an indoor greenhouse instead.

NOT REALLY.

Go ahead and regift that useful herb-gardening kit that someone offered to you.

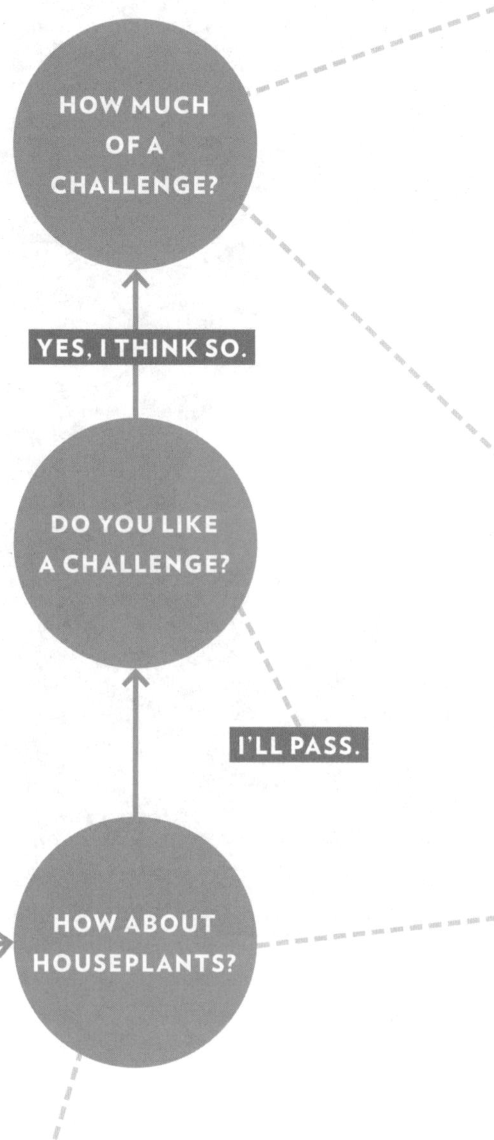
HOW MUCH OF A CHALLENGE?
YES, I THINK SO.
DO YOU LIKE A CHALLENGE?
I'LL PASS.
HOW ABOUT HOUSEPLANTS?

THE BIGGER, THE BETTER.

It's time to grab a hammer. A cold frame will give you all sorts of new possibilities, and you might as well get the full DIY experience by building it yourself. If you do it right, you can grow veggies in there even when there's snow blanketing the ground!

START ME OFF SMALL.

Try forcing bulbs indoors. Paperwhites are easy, so challenge yourself to take on something a little more difficult, such as tulips or daffodils. Even if you're not completely successful, it's nice to have something to look forward to.

NO WAY.

They cause clutter, right? Feeling that way doesn't make you a bad gardener. You merely prefer your plants to be outdoors.

THEY'RE LOVELY.

Step outside your comfort zone and grow a unique or funky houseplant. Entire books are dedicated to this subject; go to the library and check one out.

ALL "NO" ANSWERS? SORRY TO HEAR THAT! YOUR BEST BET IS SIMPLY TO DREAM OF SPRING.

Morning glory

Field Notes

Glory days

Morning glory vines take over my deck every summer. I appreciate them in all their simple beauty as the sun shines brightly on them and bees buzz around.

—Lori Hayden
Louisville, Kentucky

Houseplant Hacks

A few passionate green thumbs share tried-and-true tricks for success with gardening indoors.

When my inside potted plants are dry, I put ice cubes on top of the soil to slowly melt and water the plant without flooding the pot. It's easy, there's no mess, and I'm less likely to overwater this way.

—Lisa Sherman
Carlsbad, California

I water houseplants with water I've boiled eggs in. It works better for me than any commercial plant food!

—Sandy Lewis,
Akron, Ohio

I read that sprinkling the dirt with cinnamon prevents powdery mildew, so I gave it a shot—it worked! I no longer have a problem with the disease.

—Jeanine Buettner,
Kalispell, Montana

Collect rainwater and use it on your houseplants. I've been doing it for years!

—Sharon Woodworth
Georgetown, Kentucky

Always check with a moisture meter before watering.

—Louise McVay
Waleska, Georgia

Move houseplants outside in summer. They love rain, heat and humidity. Bring them in before first frost and spray any insects with an organic insecticide to prevent the bugs from moving into your home.

—Lynn Jones
Salem, Indiana

Fawn

PESTS BE GONE!

Discover natural ways to keep backyard bugs, slugs and animals away from feeders.

◀ CURIOUS DEER
Consult lists of the most pest resistant plants, and avoid or remove ones that attract deer, such as tulips, pansies, hostas, arborvitae and yew.

The only real way to avoid deer altogether is an 8-foot-tall fence of plastic-net deer fencing around your vegetable garden or yard. If bunnies are your bane, a 4-foot-tall wire fence will do; just be sure to bury the bottom 6 inches to prevent them from digging under it.

RONALD WITTEK/AGE FOTOSTOCK

When Trouble Hops Along

If bunnies are a burden in your garden, here are a few quick fixes.

- Call local authorities to find out whether live trapping is legal in your area.
- Surround your trees with a layer of hardware cloth at least 4 feet high.
- Remove any signs of rabbit nests to help control the population.

Deterrents are worth a try and are best used before furry pests are a problem. Hang bars of strong-scented soap or use homemade garlic spray. You can also apply blood meal or repellent granules around plants, or spray them with commercial products to make them smell and taste bad.

▶ **SORRY, RABBITS!** Try planting just out of reach. Grow flowers and veggies in containers on a porch or deck, away from deer and rabbits. Keep pots away from railings and steps, as deer stand on their hind feet to browse.

Periodically move the feeders by 3 or 4 feet. Birds will still find them easily, but insects often won't.

Set a trap by placing boards in shady areas of the garden where slugs and snails hide in the daytime. Lift up the boards and scrape off the pests. You can do the same thing with inverted grapefruit rinds in problem areas.

▼ SNAIL BAIT

Bury tuna fish cans or plastic yogurt cups in the dirt up to their rims, then crack a beer and fill the containers (the older and more stale the beer, the better). Slugs and snails are attracted to the yeasty aroma, then fall in and drown. You can replace the beer as needed.

EVAN SKLAR/GETTY IMAGES

Wandering snail

Fake wasp nest

Plan to be Pest-Free

Use these simple and easy techniques to keep your yard safe from bad bugs and pesticides.

BLAST THEM.
Dislodge aphids and mites with a blast from the hose.

LATHER UP.
Shake adult Japanese beetles off plants and into a soapy jar of water.

REMOVE IT.
Other than small-scale infestations, it's usually easiest to destroy the plant.

WELCOME PREDATORS.
Encourage lady beetles to visit and eat aphids and spider mites.

PICK 'EM.
Remove larger pests like squash bugs and tomato hornworms from plants and dispose of them.

◄ **FAKE IT**
Hang a few fake wasps' nests in protected areas to deter real wasps, which tend to be territorial and won't typically venture into a place they think is already occupied.

Hang feeders with fishing line, which is too thin for ants to climb.

Attach an ant moat, typically about 3 inches wide and 1 to 2 inches deep, above jelly and sugar-water feeders. Because ants can't swim, water is an effective deterrent. Make moats or buy feeders with moats built in; keep them clean and filled with water.

ABD/SHUTTERSTOCK

Choose red saucer feeders. With their long tongues, hummingbirds can reach the nectar—but insects can't. Plus, while hummingbirds prefer the color red, bees are attracted to yellow.

▼ GUARD DUTY

Slip nectar guard tips over hummingbird feeder holes. The nectar guards block insects such as yellow jackets, but hummingbirds can still get to the nectar. You can buy them or create your own mesh guard out of an onion bag.

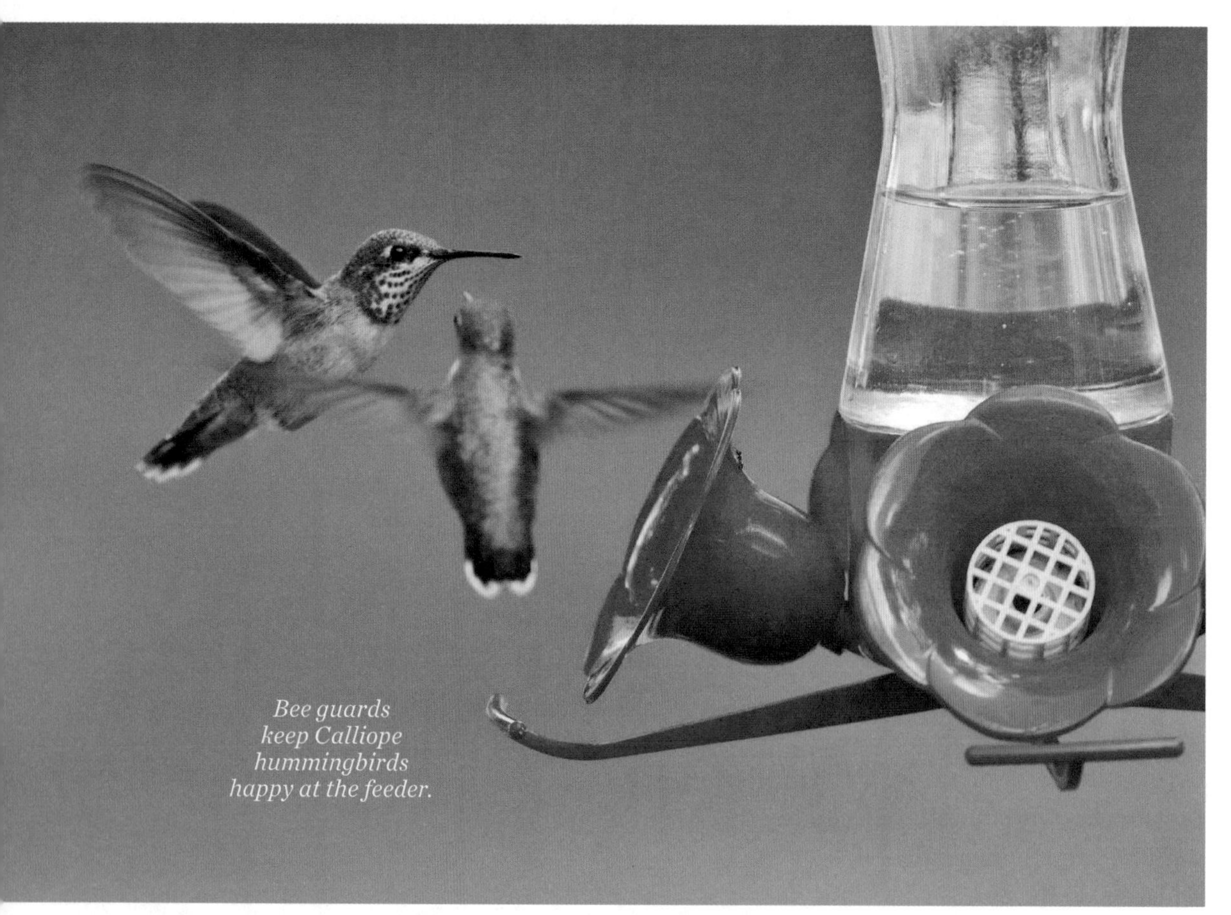

Bee guards keep Calliope hummingbirds happy at the feeder.

CHRISTINE HAINES

▲ TEMPTATIONS

Plant bee- and hummingbird-friendly food sources in hanging baskets and in your garden. Try annuals such as fuchsia and impatiens, and perennials such as trumpet vine, bee balm and milkweed.

"Half the interest of a garden is the constant exercise of the imagination."

—MRS. C.W. EARLE

STEVE LASLEY

Monarch butterfly on buttonbush